PETRA KELLY
FIGHTING FOR HOPE

Introduction by Heinrich Böll
Translation by Marianne Howarth

South End Press

Library of Congress Card Number: 84–050680
ISBN 0-89608-216-4 paper

Phototypeset by Wyvern Typesetting Limited,
Bristol, England

South End Press, 7 Brookline Street #1, Cambridge MA 02139-4146
05 04 03 02   2 3 4 5 6

CONTENTS

I dedicate this book to my sister Grace Patricia who died of cancer at the age of ten and whose suffering brought me into the anti-nuclear movement, and to my 78-year-old green grandmother, Kunigunde Birle, who has always been at my side in support and solidarity.

PETRA KELLY

Note to the Reader

This first edition of *Fighting for Hope* unfortunately includes a number of grave translation errors, resulting from communication difficulties between the book's British publisher and the author. We at South End Press and Petra Kelly regret this edition's choice of "mankind" over "humankind," "liberty" over "liberation," and "sexual fidelity" over "eroticism." The use of sexist language and excerpts that shorten and/or take out of context many relevant sections of the book are contrary to South End Press policies. Because we feel that Petra Kelly's work is important and the author feels that the book should be made available to U.S. readers sooner rather than later, we are distributing this first edition, prepared in England.

SOUTH END PRESS

INTRODUCTION by Heinrich Böll

A FEW LITTLE WORDS WE KEEP HEARING – AND A FEW
words about them.

First: 'changing the system'.

Every new law means a change to the system. So the people
in parliament and the legislature are the ones who really change
the system. M. Mitterand is changing the system, Sr Gonzalez
will be changing it, Mrs Thatcher has changed the system
to considerable, not to say sledge-hammer, effect. In Czechoslovakia a change to the system was sought, and stifled.
President Reagan is currently making sweeping changes to the
system. In Moscow, nothing changes; while in Peking, there is
a change to the system almost every year. So why should we be
upset when this label is applied to us? We should not be afraid if
we are accused of 'changing the system' – nor afraid of the
word 'street' either. In the course of parliamentary history,
quite a few issues have made their way from the street into the
debating chamber, become law and changed the system. Those
all too leaden rituals of change, and the 'art for art's sake' of
parliamentary polemics, can really only be set in motion from
the street. Extra-parliamentary activity is an important part of
the parliamentary system, even if only in sounding the alarm.

Major changes, not yet fully recognised or analysed, are
taking place within the vast terrain which I call the work system,
or the world of work. So when Herr Blüm says that currying
favour with the Greens is a betrayal of the working class, he
may well be making a huge mistake. It could, indeed, prove
dangerous to encourage false hopes among working people of
jobs in the traditional sense – much more dangerous than to
admit, as the Greens do, that work is scarce and likely to remain
so. A tentative formulation might be that there is little work but
a great deal to be done.

Clearly, the traditional character of concepts such as work,
workers and jobs is changing – the new proletariat is to be
found in the universities and colleges. Pausing to reflect on this

does not make you into someone who is changing the system. But it does mean you are trying to identify the changes already taking place within the system. And those who condemn the alternative society out of hand, or criticize its members because they may be receiving social security, should find out to what extent industry and other established bodies in society are subsidized, and they should then work out how little this means in terms of jobs reprieved. When the steel industry or the car industry – both of which have been held up as key industries – are run down, it is quite appropriate to wonder whether the lock still works and the key still fits. People should be in no hurry to scoff at 'alternative' ideas.

If you want to get down to things but cannot find anything to get down to, jovial invitations to roll up your sleeves are no help at all. A revolution verging on an explosion is taking place at the heart of the system, and before rushing to conclusions, we need to find our way to a new way of thinking. Who is working to change the system in Detroit, *the* car industry town? Apparently, conditions there are appalling – my information about Detroit's decline comes not from *Pravda*, but from the *Neue Zürcher Zeitung*, the newspaper least suspected of left-wing bias in all of this hallowed continent. (Indeed, are there people at work changing the system, or is the system perhaps changing itself?) As we all know, the United States is absolutely teeming with Communists – they have even wormed their way into the upper echelons of the Roman Catholic hierarchy – so we are forced to conclude that whole hordes of Communist agitators are at work, whispering in the good American people's ear, 'Don't buy a new car,' so that the system will collapse. But those wicked people who do not buy a new car probably would prefer to buy bread and potatoes (or even butter to spread on the bread, and meat to go with the potatoes), if only they had the money. I permit myself to doubt the healing powers of the free market (which, of course, is not free at all), and wonder who is actually deceiving working people about their future. There are no Reds and no Greens in power in Argentina, Bolivia, Mexico, Brazil, Chile or Peru, but these are all countries whose total bankruptcy hits the headlines daily, and where the unemployment rate has reached 50 per cent.

Just a few words about the most insane system of all, the arms system, which every day reveals its absurdity anew. We have no desire to be utopian, or idealistic or removed from reality, unlike the politicians who keep talking about *dis*armament, and hail it as a victory for *dis*armament when *re*armament falls by a tiny one per cent. We are talking about a stop or a freeze, and are enormously encouraged in this by the United States. Let us start with an arms freeze, and then let us see whether we can really disarm. There is a lot to be said about other systems too – the money and banking system, for example. Not even the so-called experts can make head or tail of this billion-dollar merry-go-round. Just one more absurdity after another? How much more absurdity can our minds cope with before we all go to pieces? How much technical expertise and sheer genius is being wasted on new weapons systems, which are then of no more use than a superior and very costly toy? If put to use, they spell death and destruction; if not, they stare up into the sky with a stupidity bordering on the metaphysical. And when people tell us to look at things dispassionately, then let us just take a look at the shining eyes of the military men when the new, the very new, the brand new equipment is displayed for their inspection and delectation. Eyes aglow with happiness, windswept hair, fluttering flags, music, a pathetic, emotional drum roll, and in socialist countries, all those obligatory hugs and kisses at the airports. Absurdity all around, in the work system, the banking system and the money system – where all those noughts might just as well be soap-bubbles. And not least, the absurdity of the media or information system.

The great, truly great writer, Gabriel Garcia Marquez did not talk about literature in Stockholm; he talked about the 20 million starving children in South America. I read very little about that in the newspapers, just a few vague references. The criminal absurdity of our food system, given the over-production of foodstuffs. The appalling queues at the gates of death. Everything is geared towards driving us to distraction and stupefaction. Everything is smiled away, laughed off in the vacuousness of conferences, the emptiness of summits and the hollowness of that done-to-death word, 'solidarity'. There are many other words that I could say a few words about. Perhaps the expression 'changing the system' may stand for them all. For an ungovernable situation, for inherited burdens.

A word that crops up from time to time, an out-moded item of strategic vocabulary, but all the same a word that accurately describes our situation in Germany, is 'glacis', or front line; you could call it the firing line. Glacis, front line or firing line for one or other of the superpowers. A special situation, requiring a special security policy, and one which lends the peace movement in both German states a special significance – *that* ought to be the object of German foreign and security policy, not this embarrassing smarming-up to both sides. Germany is almost united – no, not reunified – in the danger it is exposed to as a potential glacis of the superpowers. There is something else we should rediscover, something that has been turned into a nationalism of a gruesomely slippery and aggressive kind since 1870 – our patriotism. The Federal Republic of Germany really is *our* country, we have no other. It is an amazing country; its continuing stability is remarkable, a country where the number of conscientious objectors is on the increase, despite rising unemployment – politically and historically a flattering phenomenon for a German state.

Just a few more words about a few words and values currently recommended to us. For example, 'the family'. Cuts in student grants and rising rents, cable TV and, of course, the new video culture will all finally stabilise the family. It will be a real family party, not to mention an advertisers' field day. Mum will finally get that coat she has no need of, and the dough mixer she has no need of either – making your own bread verges on being an alternative occupation, after all.

I do not want to miss this opportunity of mentioning a brochure. It can be obtained for the sum of DM 3.00 – in fact, there is even a discount for bulk orders – from The German Secretariat of Pax Christi, Windmühleustrasse 2, Frankfurt-am-Main. I cannot completely guarantee that it was not written by communists, but I can to some extent. The brochure contains the second draft of the pastoral letter from the Catholic bishops in the United States on the subject of war and peace.

The changes that have been taking place in the United States, especially among American Catholics, have not really sunk in yet over here. But we should look towards America with hope as well as apprehension. Over there, security is not necessarily identical with weapons, and people have not yet surrendered to a provincial cynicism where sentimentality is mistaken for morality, as is so often the case here.

PART I The System is Bankrupt

'Eco-peace means standing up for life, and it includes resisting any threat to life ... The only people who have really understood what revolution means are those who consider non-violent revolution possible' *Philip Berrigan*

WE ARE LIVING AT A TIME WHEN AUTHORITARIAN ruling elites are devoting more and more attention to their own prospects and less and less to the future of mankind. We have no option but to take a plunge into greater democracy. This does not mean relieving the established parties, parliament and the law courts of their responsibilities, nor forcing them out of office. Information reaches society via the political parties; and the reverse process is important too: the parties and the trade unions also act as sounding-boards for ideas which first arise within society. But the formation of political opinion within the parliamentary system is undoubtedly a process that needs extending further. It needs to be revitalized by a non-violent and creative ecology and peace movement and an uncompromising anti-party party – the Greens. In a period of crisis, a conveyor-belt system between society and the remote, established parties, is required. Otherwise the real problems are evaded in the endless games of power tactics, until eventually, they become quite unmanageable.

A third to a half of the 2,000 million people in the developing countries are either starving or suffering from malnutrition. Twenty-five per cent of their children die before their fifth birthday. In the last twelve months, 40,000 children under the age of five died every day, and the trend for 1983 indicates that this shocking figure is likely to increase.

A UNICEF survey shows that less than 10 per cent of the 15 million children who died this year had been vaccinated against the six most common and dangerous children's diseases. Vaccinating every child in the Third World costs £3.00 ($4.5) per child. But not doing so costs us five million lives a year. These are classic examples of 'structural violence'. Conflict and unrest prevail, because the people live under threat of premature death at the hands of a brutal social order. For years now, social scientists studying the Third World have been saying that growth is taking place without development. Development has to meet the basic needs of the people in these societies – needs such as work, food, health, literacy and housing.

The system is bankrupt when $2.3 million a minute are spent on perfecting the machinery of destruction, whilst the means of survival become increasingly scarce. And the system is bankrupt when rational names are dreamed up for everything irrational. We are told that we have a ministry responsible for our security. It is called the 'Ministry of Defence'. However, there can be no defence for our country in the event of war. There can only be destruction. So why not call it by its proper name, 'Ministry of Destruction'!

'Security policy' has led us into the most dire insecurity the world has ever faced. The politics of nuclear confrontation imposes a brand of insanity upon us which runs, 'In order to defend freedom, we must be prepared to destroy life itself.' Or put another way, 'If you threaten me, I'll commit suicide.' Every day the United States and the Soviet Union add new weapons of mass destruction to arsenals which already have the equivalent of three tons of TNT in store for every man, woman and child in the world. The system is bankrupt when the politicians and generals gaily term this lunacy 'MAD' – mutual assured destruction.

The system is bankrupt when humanity shrinks from recognising that it is in the process of destroying itself. As Sam Keen of Harvard has put it, while we continue to sit tight on our stocks of nerve gas and nuclear weapons, we are all members of a sect committed to irrational violence. The enormous expenditure of energy, scientific sophistication and wealth on the military is the main cause of poverty, inflation and despair in the world.

The system is bankrupt when micro-electronics undermines the deterrent model. Missiles with a target accuracy of fifty metres can launch a direct attack on the opponent's arsenal. Thus they no longer operate simply as a deterrent, but should be regarded as weapons of nuclear attack. The microchip has made the manufacture of first-strike technology possible, and made it seem rewarding. According to the peace researchers of the Club of Rome, the world should be less alarmed by the overkill potential of the superpowers, than by the threat resulting from the sophistication of new control systems.

The system is bankrupt when doctors have to issue warnings against nuclear war, when they have to publish statements in full-page advertisements about the consequences, immediate and long-term, of a nuclear blast. Doctors have been drawing attention to the fact that there is no effective remedy for the multiplicity of illnesses and injuries caused by nuclear war, especially where radiation sickness is concerned. None of the precautions for the event of nuclear war, whether draft legislation or civil defence, can change any of that.

The system is bankrupt when more than 3,000 accidents are reported in American power stations in one year. In our view, there is no such thing as a minor incident in a nuclear power station. Clearly, 'minor incidents' can add up to a very grave danger. The system is bankrupt when it costs approximately £50 million ($75 million) to shut down a nuclear power station, and the electricity companies tell us that once a nuclear power station has been shut down, the residual radioactivity does nobody any harm, and very soon green fields will grow where nuclear power stations used to be.

After ten years of Social Democrat/Liberal government in West Germany, those of us who stood outside the Chancellor's office with tears in our eyes and lighted torches in our hands on the night of Willy Brandt's election victory are now having to face facts: not even the smallest step has been taken towards reform, towards greater democracy. Our illusions are dead and gone. We do not believe a word the established parties have to say any more. We shall not be carrying any more torches for them. We only trust ourselves now. To people who advise us to 'Go East, if you don't like it here,' we say East German principles apply in our country too. There is minimal provision for the poor and less and less of an opportunity to speak out. The system is the same; the differences are only of degree.

The system is bankrupt and nothing is certain. As Marie-Luise Kaschnitz's poem says,

> Whether we will escape without being tortured
> and die a natural death,
> or will be starving again
> and searching the dustbins for potato peelings,
> or will be herded together in packs,
> we have seen it all before.
> Will we steal away in time
> to a clean bed or will we perish in a
> hundred nuclear strikes?
> Will we succeed in
> dying with hope?
> It is uncertain,
> nothing is sure.

PART 2 The Greens and Parliament

WE CAN NO LONGER RELY ON THE ESTABLISHED parties, nor can we go on working solely through extra-parliamentary channels. There is a need for a new force, both in parliament and outside it. One element of this new force is represented by the anti-party party, the Greens. It has become increasingly important to vote for what one believes to be right on the basis of content, rather than wasting one's vote on lesser evils. The debates conducted in the established parties about the Greens are a shocking revelation of their inability to address themselves to new questions of survival. We demand a radical rethink of all the fundamental issues facing society on the part of the established parties, and this must be a condition of any talks with the Greens.

Within the peace movement, independently of the established parties, we voice the needs of those no longer able to express their concern for a peaceful and environment-conscious future through the established party system. However, a movement operating exclusively outside parliament, does not have as many opportunities to implement demands, say, for a new attitude to security, as it would if these demands were also put forward in parliament. Despite the great autonomy of the peace and ecology movements, it seems to me that they have no option but to relate to the political system as it is, given the nature of power in our society.

At the moment, the party system is still the main mechanism for selecting and deciding which issues figure on the political agenda. Consequently it is imperative, I believe, for many people in the ecology and peace movements to push themselves to the forefront of the party political stage. At the same time, we know that these movements can only be effective if autonomous bodies and local action groups continue to proliferate both within and outside parliament. We need more grass roots organisation: rank and file groups in the trade unions, alternative media, the peace movement and its members in the Green party.

We aim for a party system that is truly representative, with no entry restrictions. Right now, there is a very real need for an anti-party party, a new kind of party, which will genuinely espouse the cause of the weaker members of society, old people, the handicapped, women, young people, the unemployed and foreign workers and their families. The aspirations of the peace and ecology movements should be represented within a political forum, in addition to their expression outside parliament.

As Greens, it is no part of our understanding of politics to find a place in the sun alongside the established parties, nor to help maintain power and privilege in concert with them. Nor will we accept any alliances or coalitions. That is wishful thinking on the part of the traditional parties, who seek to exploit the Greens to keep themselves in power. The very last thing we seek is to use Green ideas to rejuvenate any other political party. The way the Social Democrats (SPD) have courted the Greens simply demonstrates the arrogance of power and underlines their sterility of vision. The environment, peace, society and the economy now pose such a threat to survival that they can only be resolved by structural change, not by crisis management and cosmetic adjustments. The Greens can make no compromises on the fundamental questions of the environment, peace, sexual equality and the economy.

We must make it clear that we will not just go away, nor will we abdicate our responsibility. Nuclear energy, the nuclear state, and the growing use of military force threaten our lives. We feel obliged to take public, non-violent action and to engage in civil disobedience outside and inside parliament, throwing a spotlight on the inhumanity of the system.

We do not want violence, not even against our political opponents. We have no wish to use the power of money or the state to resolve conflicts in such a way that someone must always lose. On the contrary, our anti-party party should encourage non-violent action as central to the new political culture.

From very early in our history, there has been radical opposition to the conventions of violence, striving for a profoundly human society, based on solidarity and the renunciation of power. Jesus of Nazareth, Martin Luther King, Cesar Chavez and Mahatma Gandhi are examples of this vision. Non-violence in the Green party represents the same attempt to unite means and ends. For us, the ends do not justify the means. You cannot do away with violence by using violence, or war by waging war, or injustice by resorting to injustice. It follows, then, that the ends are a part of the method of action, and likewise that the method of action is included in the ends. As André Trocmé once said, 'People in favour of the use of force all think that it is just a means of attaining justice and peace. But peace and justice are free from violence . . . That is the final objective of history. If you abandon non-violence, you have no sense of history. You pass history by, you put history on ice, you are a traitor to history.'

The Green party must remain a movement for non-violent change, and, at the same time, it must use parliament to make the case for non-violence to the electorate. One of the most important tasks for a parliamentary, extra-parliamentary party is to campaign for the recognition and protection of human rights. Food, health care, work, housing, freedom of religion and belief, freedom of assembly, freedom of expression, humane treatment of prisoners – all these human rights have been formally recognized by the member states of the United Nations, and all of them continue to be abused. These rights derive from a human being's right to life. Abuse of human rights can lead to the outbreak of war. Respect for human rights can help to build peace.

The Greens demand the unconditional abolition of all weapons of mass destruction. This demand is addressed to everybody, immediately and without exception, regardless of whether or when others make the same move. The destruction of mankind is the most heinous crime against humanity imaginable. There can be no justification for it or for any action which might cause such destruction.

The Greens seek a new life-style for the Western world, as well as in their own personal lives. They would like to see an alternative way of life without exploitation, and they aim for non-violent relationships with others and with themselves. The reaction of the public and politicians to the points contained in the Greens' extra-parliamentary programme comes as no surprise. The right preys upon a growing fear of conflict, as the old order is on the verge of collapse. And the left, so fixated on macro-structures, has simply failed to recognise how politics has spilled over into the 'private' sphere. An urgent need has arisen, not for material things, but for new relationships between the sexes and between the generations, as well as within them, relationships free from fear and based on mutual support. We should muster some solidarity, some friendship, in the face of our throw-away life style. More important than material goods, is enhancing the quality of life and living in harmony with the need for the preservation of nature and cyclical renewal. This is one of the most important objectives that the Greens are working for in the new political culture.

However, there can be no future for the Greens if they go in for gaining power in the same way as the established parties. The Greens are ready to work with others if the demand that parliament should speak the language of the people is finally met. So far, parliaments have acted simply as the executive body of the bureaucracy in the ministries, especially where important proposals such as airports or nuclear power stations are concerned. The Greens take a different view of parliament. We believe that parliament must represent the interests of the people, including minorities.

Parliaments have proved themselves incapable of responding to the demands of local action groups. The Greens believe that part of the work of parliament is to conduct hearings and committees of enquiry in public and to make them open to everyone. We aim to democratise parliament as much as possible putting the issues, and the costs of solving them, squarely before the public. We must set ourselves uncompromising programmatic objectives in order to stimulate debate and discussion inside and outside parliament. A place in parliament, together with the success of a non-violent opposition movement on the streets, should, we hope, put us in a position to shake people out of their apathy and quiescence.

We are, and I hope we will remain, half party and half local action group – we shall go on being an anti-party party. The learning process that takes place on the streets, on construction sites, at nuclear bases, must be carried into parliament.

All three parties currently represented in the West German parliament (*Bundestag*) have allowed their social democratic, christian or liberal intentions to disappear into thin air. What they have in common is a hierarchical structure making spontaneous, committed action impossible, so that politically meaningful decisions are only taken at the top and party democracy exists in name only.

Where in the party hierarchy is the housewife who knows just how difficult it is to feed a family when prices keep rising? Where is the senior citizen with a chance to speak for his fellows at last? Where is the worker with the monotonous job who can question the meaning of work? The men at the top with their fat salaries and their own way of life, not to mention the token women at their sides, lost all contact with the 'man in the street' a long time ago. They simply cannot think themselves into the fears and the worries of whole sectors of society.

After years of arduous, detailed work in the committees and working groups of these parties, many of us were driven to despair because, when it finally came to a decision, the party bureaucrats had it all their own way every time. Many established politicians claim that the Greens are drop-outs. Quite the reverse – we have stepped into the system in order to change it. The real drop-outs are the career politicians who have deserted their original professions to work their way up the party career ladder. With their secure incomes behind them, they can deliver themselves of sound advice to working people on how savings can be made to pay for yesterday's latest American missile horror.

Thus it can be seen that whole sectors of the population are not represented in parliament, nor elected to it. Representing their interests will only be the first step. Direct democracy means that we will fight for real influence for the people ignored by government. In doing so, can we expect the established parties to meet us halfway? Can we hope for a postive desire for change on their part? Given that their very structures run counter to the principles of democracy, can their representatives change their policies?

A political party must never become an end in itself, as have the established parties of the *Bundestag*. A party is a vehicle for the expression of opinion and interest. However, it is essential for these interests and the role of the party to be under constant and critical review. All too often in the past, we have seen the ways in which ready-made ideologies have led to destruction and aggression. So, as Greens, we offer no ready-made ideology. One can neither delegate nor dictate one's own understanding of life. The stories of Martin Luther King and

Mahatma Gandhi show that one is most likely to win people over through actually living by one's principles. Consequently, the function of the Green party within the peace and ecology movements is not to lead, but only to support. Parties and parliaments can only ever act as support systems when it comes to transforming the lives of entire groups of people. Looked at historically, it seems to me that the ecology movement cannot expect the unions or the Social Democrats to react other than tactically to the matters that concern us.

At decisive moments in German history the SPD has utterly capitulated to militarism. There is a blood-red line connecting their vote for war credits, under the Kaiser, with the present day. In July 1982, Willy Brandt made the following telling statement, 'The crucial thing for us, as Social Democrats, will be our endeavour to assimilate the important ideas thrown up by the peace movement and ecological groups, and to present a convincing response.' Is Willy Brandt envisaging a utopian situation where the SPD and the Greens establish a joint leftish-ecological front? He need only cherish such hopes if the SPD really aligns itself with the cause of disarmament and finally realises that ecology must take priority over the economy.

For the Greens, parliamentary work should be of benefit to our many supporters at grass-roots level; it must never be undertaken for its own sake.

PART 3　The Power of Non-Violence

WHEN WE TALK OF NON-VIOLENT OPPOSITION, WE do *not* mean opposition to parliamentary democracy. We mean opposition from *within* parliamentary democracy. Non-violent opposition in no way diminishes or undermines representative democracy, in fact, it strengthens and stabilises it. The will of the electorate is not expressed simply by putting one's mark on a political blank cheque every four years. It is expressed in all kinds of local groups operating outside parliament, in works councils and other self-governing bodies. This is the democratic infrastructure of society. Non-violent opposition is one way, among others, of forming political opinion within that infrastructure.

For example, the American civil rights movement undoubtedly had a great influence on public opinion, and significantly affected attitudes to the law among the American public and legal profession. That movement did not bring governments down; it did not spell the end of parliament or the courts; but it did seek to *change* these bodies. This was only possible because the spectacular non-violent campaigns in the streets were backed up by a much quieter approach in the institutions, the courts, the parliaments, the media and the schools. After all, every victory for the American civil rights movement meant a victory in the courts, in parliament, or in the machinery of government.

Non-violent opposition has nothing to do with passivity, and nothing whatsoever to do with the demeaning experience of injustice and violence. In contrast to violent opposition, non-violent opposition is an expression of spiritual, physical and moral strength. This strength is shown most clearly by consciously and specifically *not doing* anything which could be construed as participating in injustice. This could mean *not* obeying unjustified orders, or *not* holding back in situations where injustice is being meted out to others.

Greenpeace, for example, opposes those people who are

bent on destroying our environment, in an open, imaginative and non-violent way. Members of Greenpeace place themselves in the firing-line of the whale-catchers' cannon. They have risked their lives by taking their inflatable dinghies in under the ramps where containers of radioactive nuclear waste are dumped in the sea; they have entered areas where nuclear devices are tested; they have been brought in by the Spanish Navy and have escaped from under their noses, all in the space of a single hectic night.

Another example is the non-violent opposition in Poland. In 1981, at 7.30 every evening, the lights went out all over southeast Poland and no water was used, and entire Polish towns took to the streets. Thousands of people, their children and their dogs flocked into the town centre for about forty minutes each time. This was about the same length of time as the evening news programme on Polish television – which just happened to go out precisely at 7.30. And to emphasise their views about the military bias of the television news, many people living in the town centres put their TV sets in their windows with the screen facing the street. The military authorities had no response to make to this new form of opposition in Poland – tanks were not much use. Peaceful demonstrations – which Solidarity has been calling for in all regions – do not need leaders or detailed preparations. They are not even punishable offences; but they always succeed in putting the security forces on a state of alert. In one primary school in Posen, whole classes refused to accept delivery of parcels from East Germany; in Breslau schoolchildren came to school all dressed in black. In Warsaw, students spent their lunch-hour sitting in the corridors in silence. Solidarity banners suddenly appeared overnight on public buildings. Leaflets came down from on high, or spilt out of the litter bins in public parks. A lot of people have been wearing little coils which are on sale in electrical shops. In Polish, they are called *Opór* – in English, resistors.

Dorothee Sölle, a theologian who is active in the women's peace movement, tells of the American Plowshare 8 Campaign, in her book *Aufrüstung tötet auch ohne Krieg* (*Weapons kill even without war*). 'The Berrigan brothers, Catholics and pacifists, commit acts of civil disobedience in order to obey God. They destroy equipment and objects which pave the way to destruction in order to protect life.' She is referring to when the Berrigan brothers and eight other activists entered the General Electric Co. arms factory in Pennsylvania. They pushed past the unarmed guards and got through to the security area where they hammered on the warhead cone of a Mark 12a Intercontinental Ballistic Missile. They also poured blood on drawings, plans and other items to do with arms. Later they were arrested and charged with breaking and entering, trespass, criminal conspiracy, behaviour likely to cause a breach of the peace, creating a disturbance, burglary and inciting behaviour.

Dorothee Sölle goes on to say,

And while Reagan is giving the green light for mass production of a bomb which kills only people, leaving objects and buildings intact, Daniel Berrigan and his friends are in prison in the cause of human dignity. Perhaps we shall see a time when the prisons are so over-crowded with peace campaigners, that the judges cannot make the love of peace a criminal offence any more, when the generals learn to learn, and the bankers stop recommending arms speculation as the best deal going.

And Ingeborg Drewitz, a sister and a highly regarded writer, has called for a world-wide general strike. However, she is very pessimistic on the point, because she believes that it is easier to imagine the outbreak of a Third (and final) World War than the start of a general strike across the world.

But this possibility was indicated, on a much smaller scale, when in January 1978, the ruler of Bolivia, Banzer, was forced to yield to the pressure of the protest movement, and declare a general amnesty; more than 1300 people had joined the hunger strikes initiated by six miners' wives and their children. In the United States, there were the great non-violent campaigns for black rights, in protest against the Vietnam war, and in defence of a group of dispossessed land workers in California. New ideas on non-violent action in practice have come from workers in Larzac in the South of France, from the zone of resistance around Wyhl, and the action groups in Baden and Alsace.

All these examples show that creative opposition, in the spirit of Martin Luther King and Mahatma Gandhi, is possible. In his 1967 Christmas message, Martin Luther King said, 'Even today, I still dream that one day there will be an end to war and that men will beat their swords into ploughshares and their spears into pruning hooks, that nation shall not lift up a sword against nation, neither shall they learn war any more.' And Cesar Chavez, the leader of the American land workers' movement, has said,

We are convinced that non-violence is more powerful than violence. We are convinced that non-violence supports you if you have a just and moral cause. Non-violence gives the opportunity to stay on the offensive, which is of vital importance to win any contest . . . I don't subscribe to the belief that non-violence is cowardice, as some militant groups are saying. In some instances, non-violence requires more militancy than violence does.

Mahatma Gandhi acted in the unshakable knowledge that you do not arrive at the truth by violence, nor justice by hate, nor peace by hostility. In a world of hate, terror and tactical cunning, he placed his faith in the power of the spirit, and the superior strength of goodness, gentleness and complete truthfulness. The Green party too, should be working for more goodness, gentleness and truthfulness. We must act with our hearts as well as with our heads. Gandhi once said, 'The weapon of satyagraha turns what used to be violence into the reverse. Violence arises at the point when one man imposes his will and another man accepts it. But to refuse to bow to the tyrant's will destroys violence.' Gandhi also said that inner resistance must precede outer resistance; one must resist one's own dishonesty and cowardice, and the lies at the bottom of one's heart.

Non-violent groups and movements all over the world are faced with a dual problem. On the one hand, they are confronted by enormous military and structural violence. On the other, they discover that most people believe that using force is the surest way of getting what you want. But there has been a radical opposition to the logic of violence since the time of Jesus Christ.

The Greens must show how to resolve conflicts by regarding those who resort to violence not as enemies, but as people who must be liberated from their enslavement to violence. Practically every violent conflict or social change has proved that violence unleashes violence in return. Violent revolutions usually only mean a change of personnel at the top; the actual system of violence is only altered, never eliminated as a result.

The so-called enemy should be given the opportunity to rethink, to modify his behaviour, and to appreciate that any action we take is not directed against him as a person, but against the element of violence in his role. In this context, I would support the idea of a dialogue with the police and the armed forces, again as a means of focussing on the person, not his role in society. Calling a policeman a pig means you have already abandoned a non-violent attitude.

Time and time again, we forget all too easily that non-violent action embraces a wide and imaginative range of behaviour, which can always be stepped up. *Legitimate action* provides information on controversial issues by publishing facts that have been suppressed. Such activity includes readers' letters, signing petitions, distributing leaflets, demonstrating and knocking on doors. *Symbolic action* aims to provide slogans which can be easily understood, and which highlight typical aspects of violence in any situation of conflict. Symbolic action points the way for further opposition: vigils, silent marches, fasts, as well as more light-hearted events. Like legitimate action, symbolic action does not generally bring direct pressure to bear on the behaviour of the other side, but it does influence public awareness.

Non-cooperation with violent elements in the social system, is a basic premise of non-violence in theory and in practice. This whole concept includes legal methods of objection, such as strikes, boycotts, conscientious objection and non-acceptance of state honours, as well as *civil disobedience* – open infringement of the law on grounds of conscience. Civil disobedience is an escalated form of non-cooperation and direct action; it is the deliberate infringement of unjust laws and regulations. Those who engage in non-violent civil disobedience take full responsibility upon themselves for breaking the law on conscientious grounds. They would rather receive punishment or violence, than become violent themselves, or incur the blame for other people's violence by doing nothing.

Non-violence also means that men are reconciled to themselves, with their own species, with nature and the cosmos. In a deeper sense, disarmament means exposing one's own vulnerability. Martin Luther King's appeal to boycott the buses seemed ridiculous to begin with. Planting saplings at Gorleben also seems ridiculous, given that the bulldozers are ready and waiting to plough up the earth. We are not armed and we make an easy target, but we will not cut ourselves off from life. We have gentleness, force of numbers, freedom from domination on our side, and the solidarity to overcome all divisions. Our motto is, 'Be gentle and subversive'.

PART 4 Peace is Possible

E. F. SCHUMACHER
MEMORIAL LECTURE

'We can best help you prevent war, not by repeating your words and repeating your methods, but by finding new words and creating new methods' *Virginia Woolf*

ON 3 NOVEMBER 1983, I READ IN THE GERMAN newspapers with great shock about the warnings of the British Defence Minister Michael Heseltine, in which he made clear that the Military Police would shoot at peaceful demonstrators near the American Base of Greenham Common. His warnings led to very strong reactions on the side of the opposition and the peace movement. For it is now clear, very clear, that the laws in the Western democracies protect the bombs and not the people. The warning that the State is ready to kill those engaged in non-violent resistance against nuclear weapons, shows how criminal this atomic age has become.

Great Britain, I am told, has more nuclear bases and consequently targets per head of population – and per square mile – than any country of the world. And I am coming from a country, the Federal Republic of Germany, that is armed to the teeth with atomic and conventional weapons. I come here on this weekend to hold the E. F. Schumacher Memorial Lecture and would like to dedicate this lecture to the Greenham Common women. I dedicate a poem to them by Joan Cavanagh:

> I am a dangerous woman
> Carrying neither bombs nor babies,
> Flowers nor molotov cocktails.
> I confound all your reason, theory, realism
> Because I will neither lie in your ditches
> Nor dig your ditches for you
> Nor join in your armed struggle
> For bigger and better ditches.
> I will not walk with you nor walk for you,

I won't live with you
And I won't die for you
But neither will I try to deny you
The right to live and die.
I will not share one square foot of this earth with you
While you are hell-bent on destruction,
But neither will I deny that we are of the same earth,
Born of the same Mother.
I will not permit
You to bind my life to yours
But I will tell you that our lives
Are bound together
And I will demand
That you live as though you understand
This one salient fact.

I am a dangerous woman
Because I will tell you, Sir,
Whether you are concerned or not
Masculinity has made of this world a living hell,
A furnace burning away at hope, love, faith and justice.
A furnace of My Lais, Hiroshimas, Dachaus.
A furnace which burns the babies
You tell us we must make.
Masculinity made femininity,
Made the eyes of our women go dark and cold
Sent our sons – yes Sir, our sons –
To war
Made our children go hungry
Made our mothers whores
Made our bombs, our bullets, our 'food for peace',
Our definitive solutions and first-strike policies.
Masculinity broke women and men on its knee,
Took away our futures,
Made our hopes, fears, thoughts and good instincts
'Irrelevant to the larger struggle',
And made human survival beyond the year 2000
An open question.

I am a dangerous woman
Because I will say all this

Lying neither to you nor with you
Neither trusting nor despising you.
I am dangerous because
I won't give up or shut up
Or put up with your version of reality.
You have conspired to sell my life quite cheaply
And I am especially dangerous
Because I will never forgive nor forget
Or ever conspire
To sell your life in return.

Women all over the world are taking the lead in defending the forces of life – whether by demanding a nuclear-free constitution in the Pacific islands of Belau, campaigning against the chemical industry after Seveso, or developing a new awareness of the rights of animals, plants and children.

We must show that we have the power to change the world and contribute towards the development of an ecological/ feminist theory, capable of challenging the threat to life before it is too late. Just a few days ago the American House of Representatives agreed to go ahead with the construction of the first 21 of 100 planned MX inter-continental missiles. I have just returned from a trip to the men at the Kremlin in Moscow and to those men in power in East Germany. And this year I have been to Washington several times to meet those in power there too. And during each trip, whether it was to Moscow or Washington or East Berlin, I tried at the same time to speak with the people at grass-roots level, those struggling against the military-industrial complex whether it be capitalist or state socialist. And while I sat listening to those men, those many incompetent men in power, I realized that they are all a mirror image of each other. They each threaten the other side and try to explain that they are forced to threaten the other side; that they are forced to plan more evil things to prevent other evil things. And that is the heart of the theory of atomic deterrence.

Today our planetary environment is threatened on a scale unprecedented in human history – from the extinction of species, the build-up of toxic and radioactive waste, deforestation and desertification, to the massive alteration of the global climate. We are watching cowboy economics and cowboy threats; we are watching an industrial order with its expansionist, machismo, militaristic, and patriarchal nation states. Confronting the system of machismo is a trend towards new-age politics, a trend towards eco-feminism. We try to make others aware of such basic principles as the value of all human beings and the right to satisfaction of basic human needs within ecological tolerances of land, sea, air and forests. All these principles apply, with equal emphasis, to future generations of humans and their biospheric life support systems, and thus include respect for all other life forms and the Earth itself.

Susan Griffin wrote in her foreword to the book *Reclaim the Earth* that if there is one idea, that can be said to link together all we represent, this idea is also a *feeling*. 'It is a grief over the fate of the Earth, that contains within it a joyful hope that we might reclaim this Earth.' For what we have in common in the world-wide ecological, feminist and peace movements, is not small. In many countries all over the world, women especially are taking an increasingly prominent role in political struggles. For a growing number of women, these movements have brought about a gradual release from the constraints of traditional women's roles, enabling us to reclaim invaluable time and energy. Leonie Caldecott and Stephanie Leland have written: 'This is a slow process, and by no means a universal one as yet. However, within this process, we are gaining a sense of our strength and worth as individuals and, in a collective sense, as women.'

We must realize that the nuclear arms race is in large part underwritten by masculine behaviour. Modern science is basically a masculine endeavour and, in a world of competing nation states and military blocks, serves to fuel the fires of human conflict rather then quench them. Masculine science and masculine thinking were applied in the concentration camps of Auschwitz, in Dresden, in Nagasaki, in Vietnam, in Grenada, in Afghanistan and in Prague in 1968. The arms race, I believe, is insane, but an inevitable outcome of science in a world where men wage war against feminine values, women and nature. If we trace the myths and metaphors associated with the conquest of nature, we must conclude that humanity's long term future depends on a radical re-evaluation of masculine institutions and ideologies. And those women in power such as Margaret Thatcher or Indira Gandhi have only come into power in this male-oriented world because they have adapted themselves to male values and male ideologies.

The Women's Pentagon Action organized in November of 1980 – during which many women surrounded the Pentagon for two days of non-violent direct action against all military violence and against the sexual and economic violence in the everyday lives of all women – adopted a statement of unity expressing the diverse political concerns of the eco-feminist movement:

We are gathering at the Pentagon, because we fear for our lives. We fear for the life of this planet, our Earth and the life of our children who are our future. We have come here to mourn and rage and defy the Pentagon, because it is the work place of the imperial power which threatens us all. Every day while we work, study, love, the colonels and generals who are planning our annihilation walk calmly in and out the doors of its five sites. They have accumulated over 30,000 nuclear bombs at the rate of three to six bombs every day. They are determined to produce the billion-dollar MX missile. They are creating a technology called Stealth – the invisible, arsenal. They have revised the cruel old killer, nerve gas. They have proclaimed Directive 59 which asks for small nuclear wars, 'prolonged' but limited. The Soviet Union works hard to keep up with United States initiatives. We can destroy each other's cities, towns, schools and children many times over . . .

The very same men, the same legislative committees who offer trillions of dollars to the Pentagon, have brutally cut daycare, children's lunches, battered women's shelters. We are in the hands of men whose power and wealth have separated them from the reality of daily life and from imagination. We are right to be afraid.

We women are gathering because life on the precipice is intolerable. We want to know what anger in these men, what fear which can only be satisfied by destruction, what coldness of heart and ambition drives their days. *We want to know, because dominance is exploitative and murderous in international relations, and dangerous to women and children at home – we do not want that sickness transferred by a violent society through the fathers to the sons.*

We want to end the arms race. No more bombs. No more amazing inventions for death. We understand all the connectedness. We know the life and work of animals and plants in feeding, refeeding, and simply inhabiting this planet. Their exploitation and the organized destruction of never-to-be-seen-again species threatens and sorrows us. The Earth nourishes us as we with our bodies will eventually feed it. Through us our mothers connected the human past to the human future. With that sense, that ecological right, we oppose the financial connections between the Pentagon and the multinational corporations the Pentagon serves. Those connections are made of gold and oil. We are made of blood and bone, we are made of the sweet and finite resource, water. We will not allow these violent games to continue. *If we are here in our stubborn thousands today, we will certainly return in hundreds of thousands in the months and years to come.*

And so, together with my sisters in Greenham Common, we demand an end to the arms race and an end to interventionist policies in the Third World. As women who learn to care for life and to ease conflicts, we know that violence solves nothing. We know that everything is connected. Violence, oppression, domination, are all related ways to keep the powerless in their place. The same racism that fuels United States war-mongering in El Salvador and Grenada makes it impossible for blacks and Indians to find jobs or get decent schooling. The same machismo that breeds wars also encourages rape, pornography and the battering of women. There can be no peace while one race dominates another or one people, one nation, one sex despises another.

Jessica Fiedler of Iowa was one of three children and several experts on child development who testified before the Select Committee on Children, Youth and Families. She said, 'I think about the bomb just about every day now. It makes me sad and depressed.'

In a typically helpless male way, one of the members of the House explained that this Committee Hearing on Children's Fears of Nuclear War was being held in order to better understand the behaviour and the hopes and aspirations of children. Several Republican Committee members objected to the Hearing. 'Defense policy is not a proper subject for this Committee, even if their policy is articulated by children,' stated one of the members. But what is so frightening is the fact that surveys have been taken in which 80 per cent of the students polled said they thought there would be a nuclear war in the next twenty years. And 81 per cent said the threat of nuclear war affected their hopes for the future.

Recently reading the summary of the Office of Technology Assessment on the Effects of Nuclear War, I have come across some of the most absurd facts and opinions ever presented, such as that the seasons of the year have a direct effect on the population death during nuclear war. The 'competent' men in power explain that an attack in the dead of winter might not directly damage agriculture but may lead to greater death from fallout radiation, cold and exposure. The study becomes even more absurd when it explains that we have not yet found a solution to the control of fires during nuclear wars, because of the blast destroying all fire stations, as happened at Hiroshima. Those same high men in places of power explain that there is no reliable way to estimate the likelihood of such effects. In fact they question openly the physical and psychological vulnerability of a population during a nuclear attack. The study states,

'Even more critical would be the events after the attack ...
Assuming that war ends promptly, the terms on which it ends
could greatly affect both the economic condition and state of
mind of the population.'

And if you want more irony, read on: 'The post-attack
military situation could not only determine the attitude of other
countries, but also whether limited surviving resources are put
to military or to civilian use.'

As you see, those men in places of power are worrying about
whether or not the remaining survivors are put to military or to
civilian use. So the children of the World have good reason to
tell their fears of nuclear-age life.

Philip Berrigan, a dear friend of mine and a friend of the
Green Party, has made the following comment:

We are moving in the direction of mass suicide and total annihilation,
all in the name of legality. But governments are continually breaking
the law at national and international level. These governments behave
in an illegal and uncontrolled manner. Without the cloak of legality,
they could not carry out this atomic insanity. And for that reason, we
must call our actions non-violent civil *disobedience*, though they are in
reality civil *obedience*.

We, the Green Party, are not only indicting the Federal
Government; we are indicting *all* the governments of *all*
nuclear powers, whether it be the United States, the Soviet
Union, Great Britain, France, China or India – as well as all
states which are secretly acquiring atomic weapons through the
civilian nuclear fuel cycles. We indict the nuclear powers,
because their willingness to use atomic weapons removes the
very foundations of international law and human rights;
because their threat to use such weapons infringes the general
rules of international law; because they have not observed their
accepted obligation to effect nuclear disarmament; because the
advances in weapons technology without any political controls
make an atomic war inevitable, and thus nullify the fundamen-

tal right enjoyed by all living and future human beings to their existence and their security.

We know that the Greenham Common women have gone to Court in the United States. In 1981, the Green Party also lodged criminal charges against Helmut Schmidt and Hans-Dietrich Genscher for their betrayal of peace and for 'preparing a war of aggression'. The German Penal Code states with reference to the betrayal of peace: 'Anyone who prepares a war of aggression in which the Federal Republic of Germany is to take part and thus precipitates the danger of a war for the Federal Republic of Germany, is liable to a punishment of lifelong imprisonment or a term of imprisonment of not less than ten years.' In February of this year, 1983, in Nuremberg, the Green Party held a Tribunal against First-Strike and Mass Destructive Weapons. We made quite clear during that Tribunal, that we, the people, must put on trial the political and military leaders who are dragging hell into the Earth. We must reverse this trend if there is to be any security. Today the arsenals of the atomic powers have the explosive power of well over one million Hiroshima bombs. Nuclear superiority is completely meaningless when so many thousands of weapons are already in existence. The balance of terror is also meaningless when each side can kill the other ten or twelve times over.

The United States now has 9,500 strategic nuclear weapons, and the USSR has about 7,700. There is a rough equality between their strategic arsenals. No defence against these weapons exists. Neither side, now or in the foreseeable future, can disarm the other in a successful first strike.* At present, NATO doctrine includes the first use of tactical nuclear weapons to repel a non-nuclear attack. The use of such weapons on the battlefield could swiftly escalate to all-out

* Thus first-strike weapons such as Pershing II, which can 'decapitate' the other side, are now to be deployed, creating a second Cuba Crisis in Europe!

nuclear war which would devastate much of the Northern hemisphere. The NATO alliance has the manpower, economic wealth and technological prowess to mount an adequate conventional defence against a non-nuclear attack by the Soviet Union. This is confirmed by US General Kroesen, who has stated that NATO need *not* resort to any nuclear weapons in case of a non-nuclear attack. Nuclear war is most likely to begin as an outgrowth of conventional war, through miscalculation, through errors in computers, or as an act of desperation. The advent of more threatening, more precise, nuclear weapons heightens the risk of an attempted pre-emptive attack. Most of the new nuclear weapons are less verifiable, making arms control treaties even more difficult to achieve. We have asked for a long time that NATO should announce its intention to adopt a policy of no first use of nuclear weapons in Europe. The United States must also announce its intention to adopt a policy of no first use of nuclear weapons elsewhere in the world. And we feel that all nuclear powers, including France and Great Britain must immediately sit down at the negotiating table placing all sea-, air- and land-based systems on that negotiating table and start honestly reducing their arsenals. The zero option as put forth by Ronald Reagan is a completely hypocritical one, for it ignores, in dealing with arms reduction, all the existing NATO weapons on our side. It asks for the removal and scrapping of SS 20s, SS 4s, and SS 5s, while NATO is not prepared to reduce any existing nuclear weapons on our side – except for some of the old ones they are about to replace anyway.

We have demanded that the British and French potentials be counted, for even in the White Book of our Defence Ministry of 1979 they were counted as part of the NATO package. Many of you know that the highest NATO commander has powers of decision-making as regards those potentials in Europe. The Congressional Study of the Library of Congress of the United

States has also demanded that the British and French nuclear forces be counted in the INF negotiations. The proposals of Mr Andropov could thus lead us out of the nuclear dilemma. We are asking, as we have asked in Moscow, that Mr Andropov and the men in the Kremlin go far beyond those proposals: that is to say, they should initiate unilaterally their proposals whether or not there is a successful outcome in Geneva. We have asked that the Soviet Union begin dismantling their SS 20s down to the balance of terror which existed in 1979. They should start unilaterally scrapping and dismantling SS 20s while the talks in Geneva are still being held up to 17 November. We feel that this is not a threat to their military security for they are still in possession of many other types of nuclear weapons.

We in Western Europe as part of the European peace movement, are doing everything possible to stop the deployment of the American missiles, through civil disobedience and active non-violence. We are drawing distinctions between what is legal and legitimate, and we maintain that certain illegal non-violent acts may be legitimate as a last resort against the morally wrong decisions made by our governments. We realize that legal rights and moral rights are not always identical. At this time we feel that we have a citizen's duty to disobey! We feel that non-violent civil resistance to the deployment of the NATO missiles is morally correct, because these weapons create an irreversible new situation leading us to war and reducing the chances of survival of future generations. We realize that by engaging in civil disobedience we are breaking the law. Non-violent action attempts to provide an answer not only to the question, 'What do we do if the Russians come?' but also to the increasingly urgent question, 'What do we do if the Americans stay?' We are against *all* foreign troops in the countries of the World. We ask the Soviet Union to leave Afghanistan and the Americans to leave Grenada.

We must find a way to demilitarize society itself if we are to succeed. And so we must deny votes to the proponents of rearmament. We must organize alternative production in the arms industry and move towards the production of socially-useful goods, and we must organize political strikes and war tax boycotts. We want to change the structures and conditions of our society non-violently and move towards a system of social and alternative defence. We declare ourselves responsible for the security policies within our own immediate surroundings.

At a time where one fourth of all the world's nations are currently involved in wars and where 45 of the world's 164 nations are involved in 40 conventional and guerrilla conflicts – in a world where over 4 million soldiers are today directly engaged in combat and where about 500,000 foreign combat troops are involved in 8 conflicts and at a time when the United States, Great Britain, Germany, France and the Soviet Union are major arms suppliers to about 40 of those nations at war – I would like to leave you with these words:

O sisters come you sing for all you're worth
Arms are made for linking
Sisters, we're asking for the Earth.

Gandhi has stated that non-violence is the greatest force man has ever been endowed with. And love has more force and power than a besieging army. The power of love, as Martin Luther King said, is 'passive physically, but active spiritually . . . the non-violent resister is passive in the sense that he is not physically aggressive toward his opponent, but his mind and his emotions are constantly active, constantly seeking to persuade the opposition.'

These spiritual weapons do what guns and arms only pretend to do – they defend us. These spiritual weapons can bring about, I believe, the kind of social force and the great social change we need in this destructive age.

PHILADELPHIA SPEECH

Dear Sisters and Brothers of the American and German Peace Movements in the City of Brother- and Sisterhood, Philadelphia – *we must 'disobey'*

I bring you many greetings and wishes of solidarity from the German Peace Movement and from the 25,000 strong German Green Party. We are here because it is *here* where we truly find the *roots* of the Quaker and Mennonite immigrants who came to America 300 years ago in order to escape from war and from persecution. Mr Carstens, our President with a dark past, will perhaps speak of the German immigrants who travelled to Germantown in 1683 – but will he speak of the reasons for their coming here? I believe not, for Vice-President Bush, when coming to Krefeld this summer, also ignored the true concerns of these German refugees.

Mennonites and Quakers in Krefeld were not allowed to build houses of worship. They were driven from their homes in Germany and Switzerland and often killed for their religious beliefs, which included rejection of war and of the weapons of war. The first Europeans in Germantown lived in peace with the Indians – they knew friendship to be the *only* path to true peace among people.

In a nation where administrations have repressed and oppressed the native Indians and Black to this very day, this has a very special meaning – being able to live peacefully with the Indians, having concern for the poor, having concern over the issue of slavery.

The Quaker and Mennonite communities who were tortured, humiliated and persecuted in their original homes in Europe did not rise up and kill their tormentors, they practiced the way of love, the way later taught by Gandhi, Martin Luther King and Dorothy Day!

Today, we in the peace, women's and ecology movements are trying to practice that way of love too, by first demanding *unilateral* disarmament in order to initiate a *disarmament race.*

In a world where there is an overkill capacity on both sides, admitted even by governmental leaders, there is no risk at all in unilateral measures. We are no less secure, just because instead of being able to kill one another thirteen times, we can only kill one another twelve times. Not one politician, not one military leader can justify one more missile, one more warhead or one more tank! For it makes no more sense! No one stated it better than Admiral Hyman Rickover at his last Congressional Testimony before retirement. He said, 'What's the difference whether we have 100 nuclear submarines or 200? I don't see what difference it makes. We can sink everything on the oceans several times over with the number we have and so can they.'

We must realize that it is only *we* who can stop the arms race, for the multinational companies in the nuclear plant and arms business will not, the politicians will not and the negotiators of INF and START will not. We can kill thousands, because we have all first learned to call them the enemy. Wars commence in our cultures because we kill each other in euphemisms and abstractions long before the first missiles are ever launched. Now many of us as taxpayers, as workers are related somewhere to the arms industries. This nation, America, and the Soviet Union are turning the star-spangled vault of space into a battlefield for new terrifying machines of destruction. The superpowers are, at this very moment, developing and testing weapons to be placed in orbit about our small planet. How are we to counter first-strike missiles in Europe, jet-powered cruise missiles on submarines, Tridents, MX missiles, new nerve gas production and the Star Wars weapons pouring forth from the military establishments of both military blocs? Only by demonstrating continuous civil disobedience, active non-violence and an international solidarity that transcends national boundaries, ideologies and prejudices. In a very moving American document, that great political and human statement the Preamble of the Declaration of Independence, it is clearly stated that these truths are self-evident . . . That among certain unalienable rights there are the rights of life, liberty, and the pursuit of happiness. That to secure these rights, governments are instituted among men (and women!) deriving their *just* powers from the consent of the governed.

But what does that mean in the atomic age – where 'everything has changed', as Einstein said, 'except our way of thinking?' Can any government tell its people, those who are governed, how they are to die – whether it be through the error of a micro-chip in a missile silo, or through the present NATO doctrine of using tactical nuclear weapons to repel a non-nuclear attack?

Our Constitutional Court Judge, Helmut Simon, pointed out that legal right and moral right are not always identical. It is the citizen's duty to disobey in these nuclear times. We must disobey against the deployment of the first-strike missiles on European soil, which would create a second Cuban Missile Crisis. We must disobey against the new deployment of MX missiles (with ten warheads each!); against a continuous production of Trident submarines, 100 B-1 bombers; the continued deployment by both sides of such weapons as nerve gas, SS 20's, SS 18's, SS 19 and ICBMs! We are moving closer and closer to the brink – as is demonstrated by the Soviet crime against 209 civilian airline passengers; by policy directives in which Caspar Weinberger has instructed the military services to prepare for fighting 'limited' and 'protracted' nuclear wars; by the increased risk of nuclear accidents; and by the continued reliance and theories of atomic deterrence.

We also hear that the present US administration is about to scrap the Anti-Ballistic Missile Treaty of 1972, and is about to continue its horrendous voting record against peace at the United Nations.

Deployment of NATO first strike missiles – a decision first brought about through an initiative of ex-Chancellor Helmut Schmidt, will create an 'irreversible' destabilisation of international relations. NATO has manifestly and explicitly quit the phase of a *defensive* alliance and assumes the character of a military alliance with *offensive* intentions.

We, as a non-aligned peace movement in Europe, are indicting not only our own governments for agreeing to the planned deployment, but *all* nuclear powers – the USA, the Soviet Union, Great Britain, France, China . . . and all those states secretly acquiring atomic weapons. We indict also all secret police services, whether it be the KGB, the German secret service helping to initiate the violence in Krefeld, or whether it be the CIA, actively waging war in Central America.

We thank the thousands and thousands of Americans who have called for, and are organising, 'Euromissile' actions here in solidarity with the European peace movement. We are in solidarity with the men – and especially women – of Pentagon Action, Plowshare 8 and Trident Nein. For they are breaking out of the patriarchal circles of the nuclear society.

THE POISON GAS STORES
Speech to the Pirmasens Rally, 29 August 1981

'Carthage waged three wars; it was still powerful after the first, it was still habitable after the second, it was no more to be found after the third' *Bertolt Brecht*

I have come here today to support your non-violent struggle in Fischbach against Europe's largest nerve-gas store. Chemical weapons are just as dangerous as nuclear weapons, in peacetime or war. The 2,000 tons of nerve gas stored here are enough to wipe out the whole of mankind. The local communities in the areas surrounding the poison gas depots were not even informed of the dangers facing them. Even in miniscule amounts the poison causes premature ageing, leukaemia, and severe deformities in children. If one barrel were to explode, there would be enough gas to kill 300,000 people.

Storing poison gas in West Germany contravenes international law. The government loses all credibility when it makes official statements condemning chemical means of mass destruction while allowing nerve gas to be stored in its own country. One of the motives for building the neutron bomb – the preservation of factories, warehouses and docks while destroying most living organisms – has reached the peak of perfection in the use of chemical weaponry.

Material objects are not attacked or damaged at all, only people are affected. In the last few days, government spokesman Lothar Rühl said that the neutron bomb is similar in its effect to the chemical weapons that the Soviet Union has deployed in large numbers in East Germany and Czechoslovakia. In a radio interview, Rühl claimed that the Warsaw Pact's chemical weapons gave it a unilateral attack capability, and went on to assure us that NATO's nuclear capability would only serve as a deterrent, not as an instrument in a limited war in Europe.

At the moment, the peace movement in Europe is concentrating on the dangers of the new generation of nuclear missiles. But West Germany is *already* stacked to the hilt with nuclear, biological and chemical weapons. One gram of the biological weapon, botulinum toxin, is sufficient to poison several million people. During the Second World War, anthrax weapons were tested out successfully; if they had been used, Germany would still be uninhabitable today. Even if the extra American missiles were not deployed, we would still be living in danger of a nuclear, biological and chemical holocaust.

The Reagan government, in accordance with its policy of increasing defence spending while cutting welfare, is intending to make an extra $20 million available for the manufacture of chemical weapons. We can assume that similar substances for waging a chemical war are available in the Soviet Union and the other Warsaw Pact countries.

Chemical weapons and experiments in micro-biology have a gruesome history. At the end of the forties, the United States was accused of having used biological weapons to help start an epidemic among Canadian Eskimos. In the fifties the Soviet Union claimed that the Western powers had tested biological weapons in Korea. In 1970 there was a rumour that carriers of veterinary disease had been used to destabilise the Cuban economy. And it is certain that CIA-supported agents smuggled an African swinefever virus into Cuba. 500,000 pigs had to be slaughtered. A documentary in the ITV 'World in Action' series proved that chemical weapons had been tested out on American soldiers. One officer was so badly affected that he leapt out of a window to his death.

According to a confidential Pentagon study, the armed forces and other bodies regard the current arsenal of chemical weapons as old or even outmoded. Things are actually much worse than that. The missiles, bombs, canisters and containers in the nerve gas warehouse in Tooele, Utah, are leaking, or rusting or close to it, and so are the ones over here. And even worse is the fact that we have no safe disposal facilities; a catastrophe could occur at any time. If a minor, harmless road accident were to occur while chemical weapons were in transit, and a weapons container were to explode, the consequences could be devastating.

We must strive for an NBC (nuclear, biological and chemical) weapons free Europe. The United States and the Soviet Union are already working on a new generation of weapons – they are preparing the genetic bomb.

THE POLISH CRISIS AND THE PEACE MOVEMENT

On 13 December 1981 the Polish army put a stop to the development of mass democracy by declaring a state of emergency. Civil rights have been suspended; the leaders of Solidarity, who were freely elected by their ten million members, have been arrested and interned. For the last year, a constant battle had been raging between the Party and Solidarity. The Party, reduced to conservatives and reactionaries, had proved less and less able to pursue a social dialogue. More and more tasks fell to Solidarity – the authorities had shown themselves incapable of preventing the collapse of the economy or of guaranteeing essential supplies for the population. Many members of Solidarity were in favour of taking charge of the economy and the public services through democratic self-management in the factories and the country as a whole. Now, as a result of military dictatorship, the Polish labour movement has been thrown back into a situation which is actually a great deal worse than the one that existed in the summer of 1980 when the troubles began.

Whenever the military is brought in to run things, the generals always say that a state of emergency will be maintained until 'law and order prevails in the country,' until 'conditions exist for the normal operation of the machinery of state,' and until 'domestic conditions have stabilised.' The state of emergency in Poland is 'designed to rescue the country from chaos and anarchy,' according to 'UZ', the newspaper of the West German Communist Party (DKP) – but that is what the generals in Chile and Turkey keep saying too. Some in the peace movement have accused the striking workers of driving the Polish economy and the state to the brink of disaster with their strikes and demands for democracy.

Archbishop Glemp told the *Herald Tribune* on 18 January 1982, that there were subversive forces at work on both sides. One cannot dispute this statement, because organisations like the American trade union umbrella, the AFL-CIO, have been trying to influence the Solidarity movement along Western capitalist lines since 1979. On the other hand, the Polish Communist Party had become so fragmented that it could no longer turn a deaf ear to Soviet threats, and presumably General Jaruzelski imposed martial law to pre-empt an armed Soviet attack.

People in the peace movement placed a lot of hope in the forward-looking aims expressed in Solidarity's programme for workers' control and a 'self-governed republic'. Solidarity *before* 13 December 1981 inspired us all with the hope that social and political structures could be changed within the framework of the military blocs. *After* 13 December 1981 we see again that social renewal in the superpowers' spheres of influence hardly stands a chance. What, then, would happen if the Greens, pacifists, ecologists and communists were to get together and form an organized, extra-parliamentary opposition with more than 20 million members? Or imagine a revolutionary social movement is threatening the political stability of Mexico, and the ruling capitalist classes call in the military to crush the 'counter-revolution' and re-establish 'law and order' – in such an event, Ronald Reagan would be cheering for the Mexican version of Jaruzelski.

Those of us who continue to fight the deployment of new American medium-range missiles, those of us who objected to the installation of American puppet dictatorships in Turkey and Latin America, and those of us who demonstrated against General Pinochet's CIA-inspired coup in Chile in 1973 must now oppose the military crack-down in Poland.

The peace movement calls for the release of trade unionists imprisoned in Poland, Brazil, Bolivia, South Korea, Pakistan –

in fact, anywhere where people are denied their rights and are oppressed. Precisely because the peace movement is independent, it cannot turn a blind eye to Poland. Nor should we ignore the current erosion of trades union rights in Britain, where new legislation is being drafted which will make it an offence for a union to call an international sympathy strike or a political strike, punishable by fines of up to £25,000.

The state of emergency in Poland is being used to apply moral pressure on the Western European alliance partners, to bring them into line with the Reagan administration's aggressive anti-Soviet stance. It is clear to us that the United States is looking for an excuse to increase tension in order to justify its policy of intensive arms build-up. Reagan puts on a pretence of being concerned about freedom. But what about his airline pilots' strike? What about the military regime in Turkey which Weinberger has singled out as a model for the Third World? What about Pakistan and its dictator General Zia who has become a lynch-pin of security policy in the Gulf, even though he has suspended the constitution and basic rights, banned trades unions and strikes, and employs violence and torture in the prisons of Pakistan? And what about the gangster-style republics in Honduras, Guatemala and El Salvador? El Salvador is a test case for the unwavering loyalty of the allies in the conflict between the East and the West. Washington presents every form of emancipation in these politically and economically crippled states in 'America's backyard', as a communist affront.

But while on the subject of hypocrisy, we should not forget the union movement in our own country either! Solidarity with Solidarity really only takes on a political character when we pursue the same liberating objectives as Solidarity for our own country as well. Economic reform, genuine self-management in industry, truly democratic, self-governed unions, free access to the media for the forces of the alternative movement, self-determination and demilitarisation – these demands must also be voiced in Western Europe.

There is an outmoded and authoritarian structure of domination and subordination in this country too. What kind of freedom is there in the West? Freedom in the bourgeois sense: the right of the 'high achiever' to use the 'less high achiever'. Self-determination and self-government nurture faith in real freedom. They are the practical beginnings of socialism with a human face.

The best support we can give civil rights movements in Eastern European states is for the West European states to take an initial practical step towards the dissolution of the bloc system, creating space for movements in East and West Europe for social and political emancipation.

Easter marches, rallies, and peace weeks are not enough. Let's declare all towns and villages nuclear-free zones, let's initiate a disarmament race, let's take the tanks apart and produce goods that are socially useful, and let's hope that we can mount an international general strike in protest against war and militarisation, and so prevent a Third World War!

(from an essay written in 1982)

'SWORDS INTO PLOUGHSHARES':
an Open Letter to the West German Communist Party (DKP) and like-minded groups, April 1982.

'Even today I still dream that one day there will be an end to war and that men will beat their swords into ploughshares and their spears into pruning hooks, that nation shall not lift up a sword against nation, neither shall they learn war any more.' *Martin Luther King*

A few weeks ago, women in the Böblingen local 'Women for

Peace' group sent an open letter to Erich Honecker, the Chairman of the Communist Party of East Germany. In it, the women wrote, 'If politicians in the East and the West want to retain a jot of credibility, then they must stop dismissing the peace movement in their own countries as a put-up job from the other side. We expect you, Herr Honecker, to permit in your country what you praise to the hilt in ours.'

When I was in the United States at the beginning of December 1981, I went to look at the statue the Soviet Union had presented to the United Nations, on which the biblical words are inscribed, 'Swords into Ploughshares' (Micah, Ch.4, v.3). In the last few weeks, official sources in East Germany have announced that the wearing of 'Swords into Ploughshares' badges in schools or in public will no longer be tolerated. It was said that the badges had been misused to express anti-state attitudes, and membership of an illegal political organisation. People who were not prepared to remove these badges were threatened with severe consequences.

Wearing 'Swords into Ploughshares' badges in East Germany is evidence of a new awareness, and it also shows that a peace movement from below is developing and flourishing there, as it is here. We welcome this because it shows that within the corrupt framework of the military blocs, there is a grass-roots opposition to war and militarisation.

I know the official wisdom of the Warsaw Pact is that there is no need for a popular peace movement because official policy already pursues the aims of peace. There is a striking similarity between official views in the West and those in the East on this point. But the parallels go beyond that. Though the Americans have generally taken the lead in the development of nuclear weapons, the Warsaw Pact has always competed to develop weapons of its own, and the arms race has continued as a result. Any further steps, any more weapons deployed – whatever the justification – will do nothing to increase security, not even by the prevailing, and very questionable, criteria of mutal deterrent; they can only gravely endanger it. What I have to say is an objective criticism of East Germany and can be clearly distinguished from irrational anti-communism. These days the only way of telling whether people are capable of peace is by finding out whether they are capable of disarming. So why has East Germany recently tightened up its laws on conscription and military service, and why have pre-military education and training been introduced? A massive defence propaganda campaign aimed at young people has also just been launched in East Germany. It is called 'Peace must be defended – Peace must be armed', and by the end of next month the need for military strength will have been explained to meetings of members of the Free German Youth. Boys and girls in the 10th class (fifth form) will have put in a day of 'military preparedness' in order to complete their course in defence training.

In the winter holidays, younger children will take part in the 'Pioneer Friendship Manoeuvres' and air rifles will be fired and clubs thrown in the field games. I really wonder whether this is the right way to win people over to peace.

Other people have called for a 'ban on all war toys' and some were demonstrating in the Alexanderplatz in East Berlin, before they were dispersed by the police. Many people regard with disquiet the increasing militarisation of East German society, in the same way as many people here have joined us in our fight against increasing militarisation in the West.

In the current situation the East German state cannot crush the popular peace movement there, despite its warnings to the pacifists. The constant praise for peace and disarmament movements in the West, and invitations to Western writers to the 'public peace discussions' in East Berlin, are all barriers the East German state has inadvertently erected for itself. Resorting to drastic measures now would seriously undermine its credibility with the East German public and with the West.

I hope that one day all the politicians, military planners and generals in the West and in the East will come to realise that decisions about arms must once again lie within the province of the democratic decision-making process. The Western peace movement must take steps to support and encourage the peace movement in the East. We can only penetrate the logic of the blocs together, and we can only create a Europe free of NBC weapons together.

A CHALLENGE FOR THE CATHOLIC CHURCH

Religious peace efforts in the United States: impressions from a lecture tour of the United States in May/June 1982

'Misguided, short-sighted dropouts' – this is how Hans Mayer, the chairman of the Central Committee of German Catholics, has attacked the peace movement. I myself have had an uneasy relationship with the Catholic church, as someone who has left the Church after undergoing the discipline of a convent school and also as a member of the European and international peace movement. The Catholic Church in this country is still very rigidly organised and often takes a distinctly reactionary attitude on political and social questions stemming back to the days of its extensive collaboration with the Nazis.

Perhaps I would like to tell the bishops and cardinals in West Germany about some of my experiences in the United States so that they may, perhaps, appreciate the strength of pacifism in the American churches. I do wish we had archbishops here with the moral courage of Archbishop Hunthausen in the United States. Raymond G. Hunthausen, the Catholic Archbishop of Seattle, is withholding 50 per cent of his income tax as a protest against the nuclear arms build-up in the United States. Hunthausen made it clear that he was not out to divide the Christian community. And he was well aware that many people could not take the risk and the consequences of refusing to pay taxes.

Bishop Hunthausen now describes himself as a nuclear pacifist. But he did say, in a conversation I had with him, 'in our world today it is unrealistic to talk of a conventional war – so the time is fast approaching for me to commit myself to total pacifism.'

In the meantime, the authorities in Washington have pointed out that as a result of his tax boycott the archbishop is faced with the possibility of a prison sentence of up to five years and an annual fine of $10,000 for every year he refuses to pay tax. Hunthausen himself is ready to take the criminal implications into account. He has emphasised that he has given a great deal of thought to this step and that he wishes to follow the dictates of his conscience, regardless of the threat of legal repercussions.

In a lecture at Nôtre Dame University, Indiana, Hunthausen was sharply critical of preparations for a nuclear war, which he referred to as 'the crucifixion on a global scale'. Hunthausen has said that his decision to withhold income tax was a small step back to the Cross.

In direct response to Archbishop Hunthausen's appeal, twenty-three members of the American Lutheran Peace Community have issued an appeal to Lutherans to withhold taxes.

Hunthausen wrote, in a letter to the French Pax Chrisi movement,

I was also challenged to speak out against nuclear armament by the nearby construction of the Trident submarine base and by the first-strike nuclear doctrine which Trident represents . . . I say, with a deep consciousness of these words, that Trident is the Auschwitz of our times.

John Collins, the chairman of Clergy and Laity, a federal organisation in the United States, told me, 'The Catholic church has 50 million members and is thus the largest religious community in the United States. The national Bishops' Conference has issued a very clear statement condemning nuclear weapons, but that does not mean all Catholics think the same way. John Collins also told me that nowadays Catholic bishops in the United States are publicly criticised if they support the deterrent. The late Archbishop Cooke, Cardinal of New York and Chief Chaplain to the US Army, recently said that the deterrent was necessary and nuclear weapons should be manufactured and stockpiled if that guaranteed peace. Immediately, 100 priests, professors, nuns and other leading figures in his diocese issued a statement saying that Archbishop Cooke had gone against Christ's message. There were even demonstrations outside his cathedral.

The Berrigan brothers are also symbols of the religious opposition to the arms build-up in the United States. The two brothers and six other activists, men and women, were recently given long prison sentences for damaging nuclear warheads in a General Electric Company weapons factory in Pennsylvania.*

In 1968 the Berrigan brothers forced their way into a Draft Office in protest against the Vietnam war. They poured their own blood and napalm over 400 sets of draft papers and then burned them. The group prepared themselves for this action by fasting and meditating. While they were burning the papers, they sang hymns and recited psalms. Both are Catholics. Daniel Berrigan is a Jesuit. Philip Berrigan used to be a member of the monastic order of St. Joseph. They are also radicals, inspired in their non-violence by a quotation from Henry Thoreau, 'Dissent without civil disobedience is consent!' They break the rules of society in a conscious and carefully planned way.

* See above p. 29

The authorities have to react. Arrests have to be made, there are court cases and prison sentences for priests, there is news coverage and publicity. The Berrigan brothers say, 'Our humanity can only be preserved if we break down the ghetto of definitions surrounding us. Human beings should never be simply what is expected of them.' They see what they are doing as an extension of their church services. The Catholic tradition is full of symbols and gestures: ashes, water, blood, processions and pilgrimages.

Molly Rush is soon to become a grandmother. She runs the Thomas Merton Center in Pittsburgh, a parish centre for justice and peace. She was with the two Berrigans and six other activists when they broke into the General Electric factory and damaged the nose cone of an intercontinental ballistic missile with a hammer.

Molly Rush said afterwards, 'Whether the bomb is dropped or not, we have already robbed ourselves and our children of a future. At the very least, we must get the future back into our lives. Even if we cannot stop the bomb, we can still regain our lives by refusing to have any part of it.' When asked what drove her to the General Electric factory, she replied, 'A refusal to subordinate myself, a refusal to accept the deep despair that underlines the reality of everyday life.'

She went on,

The prophets Isaiah (Ch.2, v.4) and Micah exhort us to turn our swords into ploughshares . . . In confronting General Electric, we sought to obey God's law of life, not the large concerns' call for death. The way we turned swords into ploughshares is a way of fulfilling the Bible's message today. We base our action on a deep-seated belief in Christ who changed the course of history by being ready to suffer rather than kill. When we take part in this kind of resistance, we are filled with hope for our world and our children.

In his defence speech, Father Daniel Berrigan said,

Today there are Jesuits in all parts of Latin America. They are my brothers. Some have been imprisoned and some have been tortured. Many of them have been murdered. The walls of our religious communities here and in Latin America are covered with pictures of murdered priests, of priests in prison, of priests who have taken action because there was something they believed in. And these pictures haunt me. And I would like someone to tell me how I can live my life in apathy when these are the images of my own age.

The Mormon Church, a symbol of America's most conservative instincts, is also opposed to the missiles. With many other church communities and bodies it joined the trade unions in a mass demonstration against the policies of 'Guns before Butter'.

The old conflict between the values of the gospel and the interests of arming the nation is coming to the fore in America, and is a subject for discussion and prayer, even in conservative circles. I was constantly surprised to find peace the topic for discussion at church discussion evenings. The subject which most concerned these meetings was the way American arms policy causes deaths in the Third World every day, and is also one of the factors responsible for the catastrophes of famine and disease.

On 6 June, I was given the opportunity of addressing the congregation of a conservative church on the subject of the European peace movement and our objectives. I was pleasantly surprised to see the minister and her husband, the pastor, wearing 'Swords into Ploughshares' badges on their white robes. It was their way of expressing solidarity with all of us in Europe who support the East German peace movement.

A number of well-known Protestant leaders have also radically revised their attitudes to American nuclear policy. Following his crusade to Eastern Europe, Billy Graham, the world-famous evangelist, spoke out against the dangers of the nuclear arms race. In an interview, he said, 'If we continue the insanity of the global arms race, it will unfailingly lead us into such an enormous international conflagration that Auschwitz will seem like nothing more than a small foretaste in comparison.'

The disarmament programme of the Riverside Church in New York City, which is famous throughout the United States, is also a shining example of what a single community can achieve when it makes disarmament its prime concern. I visited the Riverside Church in December of last year and was impressed by their untiring efforts against the arms race. Attendance at the annual conference of the Riverside Church has recently risen from a few hundred to over 2,000 peace people from over thirty Federal states. The Riverside Church provides material and speakers for hundreds of ecumenical disarmament meetings in almost all the states of America, helping the disarmament debate to spread through the churches like wildfire.

The Roman Catholic Bishop Matthiessen from Amarillo, a conservative town in Texas, has strongly opposed President Reagan's decision to construct the neutron bomb. He suggested that the workforce at the Pantex works in his diocese, where the bomb will be built, think about going on strike. This is the first time that a senior ecclesiastical office-holder has encouraged his flock to refuse to work on the manufacture of nuclear weapons. All twelve Catholic bishops in Texas immediately supported his appeal.

Two other religious peace groups, the Reconciliation Federation and the American Friends Service Committee, a Quaker organisation, have set up a joint programme, the 'Nuclear Weapons Facilities Project'. They support and co-ordinate the activities of local groups in their efforts to obtain information about, and mount opposition to, the manufacture of nuclear weapons. These groups have visited shipyards, submarine bases and nuclear weapons factories to register their protest. Apart from raising ethical questions related to the manufacture of nuclear weapons, the project group has successfully collected and published material about the effects of nuclear weapons installations on health, and the economic and social costs involved for the communities concerned. One result of their efforts was the public enquiry in 1980. People living in nuclear weapons test areas, former soldiers and the widows of uranium miners gave evidence about cancer, infirmity and death in their personal lives as a result of nuclear weapons and nuclear energy.

The Reconciliation Federation actively supports the current nuclear Freeze Campaign as do the National Council of Churches, and several other Protestant churches. The issue of nuclear weapons, weapons of mass destruction, is one that must challenge our faith. The committee currently preparing the American bishops' pastoral letter on war and peace regards the moral problem of nuclear warfare as the greatest challenge our times can pose for Christians. In the view of the committee, the time is ripe for the American bishops to take a new stand on the question of the morality of possessing nuclear weapons, even if only as a deterrent. If the Catholic bishops in America do come out against the possession of nuclear weapons, in their pastoral letter due at the end of the year, it would be a signal of international import.

I still regret that Bishop Hunthausen was unable to address the Bonn demonstration on 10 June 1982. He was forced to decline under pressure from the stick-in-the-mud hierarchy of the German Catholic church. It would have meant a great deal for everyone in West Germany to hear Bishop Hunthausen speak in Bonn, to discuss the peace movement and its future objectives with him, and to find out more about the peace efforts being undertaken by the Catholic church in the USA.

The question now remains: will the churches of Europe join us in the search for peace in a nuclear age?

OPEN LETTER TO POPE JOHN PAUL II

Some reading for your visit to the Federal Republic of Germany in November 1980

'Apart from our parents, we should also respect our superiors, i.e. spiritual and temporal authority, guardians, teachers, masters and rulers. We owe respect and obedience to spiritual and temporal authority because their authority comes from God'. *Quote from a Catholic catechism for the 'religious instruction' of children, second edition, published in 1977. It is distributed in Bavaria and was recommended by the then Pope in a letter of thanks to its author.*

Pope John Paul II, you paid your last visit to the Federal Republic of Germany in 1978 as Cardinal of Cracow. Two years later, you are returning as Pope. 'I am sure that the people of our country will give you a warm welcome', Cardinal J. Höffner said, in connection with the Papal visit.

But I am wondering how we women, my sisters in the peace, alternative and women's movements will receive you. Pope John Paul II, you are the person who recently told an audience of 120,000 people, 'The one who has knowledge is the man, the one we have knowledge of is the woman'. How will we welcome you?

Catharina Halkes, a feminist theologian and lecturer at the Catholic University of Nijmegen in Holland, appalled by your pronouncements on the subject of women, described them as 'even more dangerous than refusing to admit women to the priesthood.'

And I too am appalled that you rank women as second-class Christians. In Nuremberg, where I live, women and girls in various church communities are protesting at a Holy See regulation, which you sanctioned, forbidding women church-goers from serving on the altar. The instruction of the 'Congregation for Sacraments and Services' in the Vatican is causing a great deal of bad feeling. In the passages outlining 'some norms for celebrating and revering the mystery of the Most Holy Eucharist', it actually says, 'However, women are not permitted to discharge the functions of an acolyte.' You and the Vatican are evidently seeking to ban women from serving on the altar.

Women in Brazil, Ireland, Spain, El Salvador, in fact, women all over the world, are still fighting against a multitude of burdens and disadvantages in almost all social spheres. We have had enough of being oppressed by the all-male cliques in the ruling parties, in the trade unions, and the centres of industry, and that goes for the churches too.

We cannot be indifferent to what will happen to future generations, and we certainly cannot stand by and wonder whether our children will perish in a nuclear holocaust. How can those who seem so concerned to protect unborn life treat the life that already exists in an irresponsible way?

Pope John Paul II, you have often spoken about the insanity of the arms race and the dangers of a nuclear conflict. And you know that for every tank built, smallpox epidemics could be kept under control for ten years. We could build 45,000 modest homes for every nuclear-powered submarine. And yet people are talking about our planet as a 'nuclear burnt offering'.

In all your speeches, addresses and sermons all over the world, you speak of the necessity for peace, and of the many dangers that arise from greed for profit. But there is one danger you never mention: the danger associated with the so-called 'peaceful' use of nuclear energy. Why do you only mention the bomb and leave out the reactor? Can you separate one from the other? Have you forgotten that 'peaceful' use is actually a waste product of military nuclear research, a waste product which can easily be used to develop a world-wide nuclear state, a Big Brother state? It is a waste product that will make the Third World dependent again, which can destroy centuries of tradition and culture for entire peoples (e.g. the Australian aborigines, the Indians, the Janomani in Venezuela and Brazil, the Irish in uranium-rich areas), and which secures membership of the atom bomb club! All attempts to halt the spread of nuclear weapons have failed. Eleven countries, including Brazil, Argentina, South Africa, Pakistan, Iraq and Libya have nuclear programmes, the aims of which are obscure. But with the aid of their reactors they can manufacture a nuclear bomb any time they choose – always assuming they do not possess one already.

But, Pope John Paul II, what did you say to the Brazilian government in this connection during your visit to Brazil? Did you issue a warning? We have heard nothing, Holy Father. Was your warning so soft and gentle that we missed it entirely, or did you hold your peace on this fundamental issue? Or is it no concern of the church when reactors can produce bombs, that mean Hiroshima a million times over?

It is particularly repugnant that the Vatican, the Holy See, is itself embroiled in nuclear trading!

I was at the International Atomic Energy Organisation in Vienna in October and learned that the Vatican has put its (your?) signature to the agreement on nuclear transport concluded by fifty-eight countries. This agreement is designed to safeguard the transport of nuclear material between states and also therefore to protect it from direct action by opponents of nuclear power stations.

The policies of the people behind the entire nuclear spiral are based on a contempt for mankind. It has already started where the Australian aborigines and the indigenous populations of South and North America live, and this policy will end in 'bloodless' catastrophes like the one in Harrisburg. The Vatican is caught up in this spiral. Why, I ask you, why? We women in the trans-national ecological green movement are taking responsibility upon ourselves. We engage in civil disobedience against a nuclear arms state, we demonstrate in a non-violent way with and for our children. Some women in the Greens are refusing to bear children because they can no longer take the responsibility of bringing a child into this world. We are well aware that the proliferation of nuclear and chemical industries in our society will lead to severe, long-term health and genetic damage.

Pope John Paul II, perhaps you should have been in Stuttgart on 2 July 1980 when more than fifty pregnant women with their babies and toddlers entered the Stuttgart Parliament to demand the immediate shut-down of nuclear power stations. Perhaps it would have done you good if you had taken part in the 'Christians against nuclear energy and nuclear arms' seminar in Osnabrück in July 1980. The seminar took as its starting point the belief that 'many Christians have become aware that nowadays their faith and their responsibility for life can only mean one thing: opposition to both military and "peaceful" use of nuclear technology.'

In Brazil you attacked social injustice and poor social conditions, and you warned against violence and class warfare. But even you were at a loss to know how the lot of the poor could be improved. Was your visit anything more than a fleeting shadow on the red carpets of the basilicas and across the poor districts where you met hopelessly oppressed people? Or was your visit just an effective self-promotion campaign. And were your speeches not all too ambiguous? Despite your repeated admonitions about social injustice, you failed to take a public stand on the conflict between an authoritarian state and a church which is increasingly open in its support for the demands of the poor.

Jesus Christ, whose representative on earth you are, always took the part of the oppressed and the weak. The oppressed must come first in a church which claims to follow Jesus. Money and property should not be a privilege for the few. The New Testament teaches us that a man who shares his power and money with the poor is only giving back what belongs to the poor by right. Many of us follow with close interest the new liberation theology of bishops such as Dom Helder Camara.

I have a very dear friend, a priest, who buried my sister in Würzburg in 1970 following her death from cancer. He is now living in Honduras and has turned to liberation theology. He writes and tells me of his experiences there. His letters are a clear indictment of capitalism because, like many priests in Latin America, he knows this system offers no escape for the poor. So one must think about an alternative system, one where distribution is not just seen as a problem for technocrats. The community must decide who should bear the cost for a human society. Capitalism does not satisfy even the elementary needs of the broad mass of people in Latin America, whilst it increases the wealth of the few. That is why we are looking for a new third way, a liberation theology, a comprehensive set of ecological solutions and alternatives.

Another sin by omission is the Catholic church's evasion of the subject of non-violence. Non-violence, after all, is a central tenant of the early Christian texts. We must heed Cyprian's words: 'When a murder takes place in the private sphere, it is regarded as a crime. But when it takes place with the authority of the state, it is called heroism.' And Clement of Alexandria says, 'If a man is looking for peace, he should not use a sword, nor other weapons.' Perhaps you could learn from St John Chrysostom who said, 'It is truly greater and better to change our enemies' intentions by transforming their hearts, than to kill them.'

The starting point of my letter to you was that women here

are insisting upon their place in the church, if they are not to leave it entirely.

You, Pope John Paul II, will be meeting the bishops who call us women 'murderers' and equate us with Nazi criminals for our defence of abortion rights.

But the best protection against unwanted, and therefore endangered, life is its prevention. And the same priests who profess to protect life condemn measures to prevent unwanted pregnancy. The theologian, Dorothee Sölle, has said in *Choosing Life*, 'Publicising (contraceptives) not just tolerating their use, would mean an unreserved acceptance of human sexuality which does not find its meaning in procreation. The churches still take an animal view of sexuality. And the continuing ban on contraceptives is an extension of this animal view.'

The annulment of a Catholic marriage, as in the case of Jackie Kennedy's rich sister, is really a question of class and status. Wealthy women can afford it. So statutes on abortion have become a question of class and status too; rich women can always 'buy' their grounds for termination.

May I quote you some important UN statistics? 'Whereas in the Federal Republic of Germany there is one termination for every five births, in Austria, Japan and the Soviet Union there were more terminations than births.' In staunch Catholic countries such as Uruguay, Portugal and Italy, in particular, where until recently legislation was very strict, there was one abortion, 'mostly illegal', for every birth. The Catholic church cannot just look at the increase in legal terminations and pretend that the only alternatives are legal terminations or none at all. The UN statistics prove conclusively that in countries where legislation has been relaxed and then tightened up again, there has been no reduction in the total number of abortions. In fact, the proportion of illegal abortions has significantly increased in these countries.

Women all over the world must first fight for decent human conditions before they bring more children into the world. We have had enough of living with environmental pollution, with the violence that is a feature of our everyday lives, and of living in a world that is hostile to women and children. I implore you Pope John Paul II, to understand that it is a question of women's dignity as human beings and of women's perspectives on life.

We will go on fighting together in an effort to arrive at an 'image of humankind' that is not purely the product of men. We are rediscovering a feminine spirituality, and the women mystics who, as so often happens, have been pushed into the background, hidden away and suppressed. We cannot wait any longer . . . And that is why we support every move to liberate the church and the Holy Scriptures from their sexism.

What is the real mission of the Church? Who gave it this mission? We women in the Greens reject the words of Paul the Apostle who identified man as 'the head of the woman' (first letter to the Corinthians, Ch.11, v.3) because the man is 'the image and glory of God', but woman is 'the glory of the man' (1 Corinthians, Ch.11, v.7). Paul the Apostle has provided the theological instrument with which woman has been subordinated to man within the Church.

When Christ was alive, there was no Christian Church. Jesus gave His mission to Christians, not to the Church. Christianity in its early stages became a religion of the oppressed because of His mission. ('Love is the fulfillment, all laws are contained in this.') Christianity was radical then. Christians lived in communes and sought to abolish private ownership, but this radical Christianity was destroyed. 'Radical' means 'going back to the roots', and the radical elements of Christ's message still remains a danger to those in power. What was a religion of the oppressed, the Church has made into a system that oppresses them further.

APPEAL

From Petra Karin Kelly and Hermann Verbeeck at the Nuremberg Tribunal against first-strike weapons and other instruments of mass destruction in East and West. 20 February 1983

The implication of our resolution, our decision, here for me as well as for Hermann Verbeeck, and I hope for all Green parties on an international level, is an appeal to ourselves, to all of us, to each and every individual that we finally do something. Both Hermann Verbeeck and myself have attempted in this appeal to express that which should inspire us, mobilize us, in our non-violent struggle against militarisation and nuclear proliferation.

1. We call upon countries and cities everywhere to organise tribunals, such as this one in Nuremberg, condemning weapons of mass destruction.

2. We call upon people everywhere never to accustom themselves, never to allow themselves to become accustomed, to the idea of war and the preparation for war.

3. We call upon people to renew their forces in a non-violent effort of resistance and civil disobedience. These forces are to be stronger and more far-reaching than anything which history and the world have experienced before. We must convince the old established authorities of a new enlightened authority: the power of reason, of communal awareness, of moral conscience. Never again will people be able to say, 'We didn't know.'

4. We call upon people to find their way back to the deepest spiritual dimension of all religions: love. And love demands that we accept one another, that we come together in harmony, and celebrate the differences among human beings. We must recognise that it is only within an atmosphere of freedom that individuals are able to change themselves.

5. We call upon the younger generation to put their intellec-

tual and moral power to work in an active contribution to non-violent resistance. Through this commitment to peace, even fear itself may perform a useful service by being transformed into a creative force. We need a courageous kind of fear, a vitalizing fear, which instead of making us seek the safety and security of our homes will send us into the streets. It is a loving fear which is not simply concerned about what might happen to us, but reaches out to the whole world.

6. We call upon women everywhere, our sisters young and old, for they recognize that our governments are constantly breaking the law. Governments are unable to sustain and guarantee us peace. The women at Greenham Common, England formed a living chain, a chain of human beings, around a military base for nuclear weapons. We call upon women to form a chain around the world, and further not only to resist those who say that war is inevitable, but only to love those men who are willing to speak out against violence. We invite all men who oppose violence to join us in our cause for peace; we urge them to break out of their rigid patriarchal institutions. I appeal to women not to let themselves become corrupted by male power. Emancipation is something more than a 'ticket' to serve in the army; it is not an entrance for women to militarisation.

7. We call upon people everywhere to work for peace, to forget the quiet comfort of their homes, to leave behind their fears and feeling of powerlessness, their privileges and possessions, and join us as active participants and co-workers for peace.

8. We call upon people to build and develop communities of peace everywhere. Everyone must know that without the community, survival is impossible, that for thousands of years communities of people have practiced peace, and that the community will always be there, even when one is thrown into prison and is cut off from loved ones and comrades. If you

practice non-violent resistance you are not alone: many others are always there.

9. We call upon people to join the peace movement and become active in our non-violent protest against weapons and atomic energy. It is important to know that the world powers are afraid of nuclear war. But what they are even more afraid of are people, the thousands of people who are living for that day, for the light of day when peace will finally dawn. One should also know that at present our drive for peace has already grown so strong that the powers in both East and West have already begun to change their tactics.

10. We call upon people to practice non-violent resistance in protest against nuclear research centres and laboratories, the arms industry, N B C-military bases, and other military installations.

11. We call upon people to make use of all legal, non-violent, and imaginative means or methods in order to ensure peace and justice. These non-violent methods must accord with our non-violent goal of peace.

12. We call upon people to demonstrate non-violently outside factories, military bases, industrial complexes, governmental organisations, embassies, etc.

13. We call upon people to participate in memorial peace services, and to organise silent 'stand-ins' for peace in public places.

14. We call upon governments everywhere, upon people in responsible positions, politicians, researchers, and military personnel only to act in the service of peace and to boycott those institutions which are involved in preparation for war, and in particular for a war with weapons of mass destruction.

15. We call upon all nuclear powers in the world and above all the two Superpowers to begin taking steps towards unilateral disarmament, without waiting for the other side.

16. We call upon all civilian and military personnel who work

in any of the armed forces throughout the world to consider their responsibility and to recognize their duty towards non-violent resistance and civil disobedience.

17. We call upon people to be loyal to one another, to people in both blocks, and not simply along government lines. We must preserve our loyalty to human dignity, and that means never being partial in our treatment of human rights.

18. We call upon people to oppose strongly their governments, which are all jointly responsible for nuclear armament.

19. We call for a new attitude in which public opinion will view every conscientious objector as a hero; in terms of emancipation they are heroes.

20. We call upon people to demonstrate that we have learned from the experience of the Nuremberg War Tribunal.

21. We call upon people to recognize that we do not need nuclear weapons and other instruments of mass destruction in order to exalt ourselves.

22. We call upon people to reject that blind faith which makes us quietly assent to mass suicide and nuclear holocaust.

23. We call upon people once again not to wait until it is too late to begin thinking about world peace, the peace movement, and becoming an active worker for peace.

In 1952 Bertolt Brecht wrote to people everywhere:

Mankind's memory for the suffering people have already endured is astonishingly short. Our capacity to visualise future suffering is even more limited. The worldwide horrors of the 1940s seem to be forgotten. 'Yesterday's rain won't make us wet today,' say so many people. It is exactly this hardened indifference which we have to fight against, as death is its most extreme consequence. Far too many people already seem dead to us today, like people who have already gone through that which actually still lies before them, so little have they done against this.

PART 5   There is only one World

BIOLOGICAL FARMING

ECOLOGICAL FARMING METHODS ARE PARTICULARLY economical in their use of raw materials and energy. The demand for biologically produced goods now exceeds the supply. And farmers who face ever-growing problems in keeping animals and plants healthy are turning more and more to ecological methods. However, there is a chronic shortage of places for training in ecological farming.

Farmers today, themselves the victims of the failure of agricultural policy, are often cast in the role of 'nature's enemy'. But the people who really bear the blame for the failure of agricultural policy sit unchallenged at their desks in the ministries and board rooms. The Greens do not want to see agriculture managed on industrial lines by a small number of employers. What we need is an agriculture where the backbone is provided by independent small- and medium-scale family enterprises. Farmers should remain farmers, not become agricultural industrialists.

In Holland there is widespread use of biological pest control methods and mechanical weedkillers, and cooperative depots have been established. The first organic dairies are in production and there is an Alternative Agricultural College outside Leiden. Right in the heart of Amsterdam there is even an advisory office for ecological farming (which owes its existence to the efforts of squatters, among others). In Holland there are now 226 selling points where alternative farmers and gardeners can sell their produce. In addition, the government wants to set aside a large area for small farms and market gardens working without chemical fertilisers and weedkillers. All this shows that in Holland at least, there has been a move towards the humane centres of production envisaged by E. F. Schumacher in *Small is Beautiful*.

The largest bio-gas plant in the world to date has just gone into production at Ismaning near Munich. The West German Ministry of Research contributed £62,500 ($9,400) towards the cost. When organic matter, in other words plant or animal matter, is broken down by micro-organisms in the absence of oxygen, organic gas is produced – a mixture of 50 per cent methane and carbon dioxide. In this way 4–5,000 cubic metres of organic gas can be produced every day, providing the same amount of energy as 2,000 litres of central heating oil. The gas is converted into electricity in a motor generator plant, and can be fed into the Bavarian supply network.

According to Andreas von Bülow, consumption of energy in West German agriculture is rising faster than production, because of the high degree of mechanization and the widespread use of fertilisers and pesticides. Rolf Brand, who built the Ismaning plant, has calculated that with the aid of organic gas installations, German agriculture could become largely self-sufficient in energy. There are about forty-five organic gas plants already operating in German agriculture and another thirty are currently under construction.

One important argument always put forward by our opponents is that mankind will inevitably starve if conventional farming methods are abandoned. But in fact, yields from organic cultivation are only 5–10 per cent lower. Ecological farming is not a wrong turning; it is the only way to an agricultural situation in which both the soil and the animals are healthy, and in which food is produced without risk.

As human beings, we are collective creatures, living parts of various communities which interconnect to form a living social system. Thus we are responsible for the whole, for society and for the life system that supports us all.

Most energy in the agricultural industry comes from fossil fuels, and of these, the main source is oil. Oil is necessary for the manufacture of nitrate fertilisers and pesticides. The Greens draw attention to the fact that supplies of oil and natural gas (as well as uranium) will be exhausted in one or two generations, and will become very scarce and expensive before that point is reached. We are looking for a way out of the wasteful consumption of energy in oil-based agriculture. Biological methods would give poor countries in particular a chance to liberate themselves from the mono-cultures that have been imposed upon them, and to establish their own independent means of foodstuff production. And, by using fewer artificial fertilisers, they too would see a reduction in their fuel bills.

Industrialised agriculture has a lot to do with world hunger. The rapid growth in world population will have hardly changed by the year 2000. The world's population will grow to 6.35 billion in 2000, an increase of more than 50 per cent over the figure for 1975. The gap which already exists between rich and poor nations will grow wider. On this point, *The Global 2000 Report to the President* says:

– Arable land will increase only 4 per cent by the year 2000.

– Most of the elements that now contribute to higher yields – fertilisers, pesticides, power for irrigation and fuel for machinery – depend heavily on oil and gas.

– While the world's finite fuel resources – coal, gas, oil shale, tar sands and uranium – are theoretically sufficient for centuries, they are not evenly distributed; they pose difficult economic and environmental problems; and they vary greatly in their amenability to exploitation and use.

– Regional water shortages will become more severe. In the 1970–2000 period population growth alone will cause requirements for water in nearly half the world to double.

– Significant losses of world forests will continue over the next twenty years as demand for forest products and fuel wood increases. Growing stocks of commercial-sized timber are projected to decline 50 per cent per capita. The world's forests are now disappearing at the rate of 18–20 million hectares a year (an area half the size of California), with most of the loss occurring in the humid tropical forests of Africa, Asia and South America.

– Serious deterioration of agricultural soils will occur worldwide, due to erosion, loss of organic matter, desertification, salinization, alkalinization, and waterlogging. Each year, an area of cropland and grassland approximately the size of Maine is becoming barren wasteland.

– Atmospheric concentrations of carbon dioxide and ozonedepleting chemicals are expected to increase at rates that could alter the world's climate and upper atmosphere significantly. Acid rain from increased combustion of fossil fuels threatens damage to lakes, soils and crops. Radioactive and other hazardous materials present health and safety problems in increasing numbers of countries.

– Extinctions of plant and animal species will increase dramatically. Hundreds of thousands of species – perhaps as many as 20 per cent of all species on earth – will be irretrievably lost as their habitats vanish, especially in tropical forests. (*The Global 2000 Report to the President*, Penguin Books 1982, pp. 2–3).

The structure of industrial agriculture is one of large fields, and mass application of artificial fertilisers, pesticides and high yield plants. Agriculture is currently organized on the basis of the competitive pressure to expand and intensify. But this puts a strain on the whole ecological system. In agricultural terms, pressure to expand means draining marshlands with a purpose-built excavator and plastic pipes. Alternatively, it means clearing hedgerows or ploughing right up to the hedges bordering the woodlands. We Greens must become the parliamentary representatives of the birds, the plants and the marshlands, the voice of ecological stability.

THE NEW ENVIRONMENTAL WEAPONS

An extreme case of the oppression of nature is found in the present military research to develop 'environmental weapons'. Scientists are working to produce rain, snow, hail, lightning, hurricanes, tidal waves, earthquakes and volcanic eruptions for military purposes. Between 1963 and 1972 the US military conducted 2,700 experiments in increasing rainfall, using Indo-China as their laboratory.

Numerous studies show that the production levels and standards of living in the highly industrialised countries have very little long term prospect of being maintained. Mankind is losing the basis of its existence. The biological diversity of flora and fauna is facing the threat of extinction; by the year 2000 there could well be no more trees on the streets; the springs will start to dry up and drinking water will be scarce; heavy metals and radioactivity will have contaminated the fields, breast milk and young children. The findings are extremely alarming but the reactions from the political parties so far have been very few and far between.

In the face of these incalculable dangers, more and more people are no longer prepared to tolerate economic pressures at any price. This can lead to apathy, or radicalisation and mobilisation in the ecology and Green movements. The Greens believe that current endeavours to come up with a solution within the framework of the market economy system do not go far enough. We must construct an ecological framework for the survival of life on this planet.

THE CHEMICAL INDUSTRY AND POLLUTION

According to the OECD (Organization of Economic Cooperation and Development) report, there are more than 70,000
chemicals on the market today, and 1,000 new chemicals a year
are introduced into the twenty-four OECD states. Where
chemicals are concerned, there are two things to be borne in
mind: (a) the effects of a massive dose of chemicals; and (b) the
effects of constant exposure to a small amount of any one
substance over a period of time. After all, the effect of a small
but constantly active dose could well be fatal, whereas the
short-term effect of a massive dose of the same substance need
not necessarily be so. In the field of radiation risk especially, the
evaluation of data about atomic bomb victims, workers in the
nuclear industry and patients who have received clinical radiation treatment has shown that radiation has a cumulative
effect, several small doses together having the same effect as
one large one.

Almost all countries have inadequate legislation where
chemical toxins are concerned. It will be the developing
countries which will have to bear the brunt of any chemical
catastrophes in the future. Products which are banned in their
country of origin, in Europe, say, find lucrative markets in the
developing countries.

We, the Greens, are deeply concerned about the increasing
danger to babies and children of toxins in the environment.
Their concentration in breast milk, in particular, can no longer
be accepted. To be breastfed is one of the most basic human
rights and it must not be jeopardised by the creeping con-
tamination of mothers' milk.

Politicians say a great deal about protecting children, but in
practice they do very little about it. Our environment is already

stacked to the hilt with chemical substances and toxins, quite aside from the radioactivity from nuclear bombs and power stations. An adult's daily life is already characterized by waste-gas clouds, radioactive substances and contaminated food-stuffs, but a child is exposed to a much greater degree. Children absorb chemical toxins and radioactivity into their bodies while they are still in the womb. They are born contaminated. Children are the first to be affected by environmental disasters, such as those in Japan or Seveso, and they suffer the greatest damage. We must wake up to the fact that the legacy we are leaving to future generations is a highly contaminated environment.

In this connection, I would like to quote Jörg Zink, a Green clergymen, because he puts it very clearly. 'We usually regard violence by one person against another as a crime, but an act of violence by a group of people or an individual against the lives of an unspecified number of others is not termed a crime. We must rethink our ideas on what constitutes a crime.' He goes on to say, 'Measured against an ordinary crime, what a small debt is owed, in contrast to the industrial concern which buries its toxic waste under the green grass by the wagonload, or which travels the world's oceans in a tanker ready for the scrapheap. How much guilt does a man incur when he is responsible for burdening our successors with hundreds of generators and the job of looking after our nuclear waste?'

We put this question to chemists, physicists, nuclear techni-cians, town planners, politicians and technocrats: what does it take to make you act as responsible people? How much longer can the principle of profit maximisation, and an economy that is preoccupied with minimizing costs, go on enslaving and deceiving us in a contaminated world?

A few months ago, I invited the Jesuit fathers, Philip and Daniel Berrigan to West Germany. Daniel Berrigan, working in a hospital for terminal cancer patients at the time, said,

'What cancer patients are suffering is a rehearsal for the future that is being planned now. Being with people who are dying of cancer means being with people on whom the bomb has already dropped.'

CANCER AND THE ENVIRONMENT

Arguments about the protection of the privacy of the individual are often quoted to oppose the introduction of a register of cancer cases. All of a sudden, the talk is all of the freedom of the individual, and of protection against computer invasion of privacy, when the Greens demand a register for cases of cancer in areas where heavy industry and nuclear installations are located. But the connection between cancer and industrialisation can no longer be denied. An American cancer atlas shows that lung and skin cancer are particularly common in areas where there is a high concentration of petro-chemical industries, and where iron and steel works belch out their smoke. The industrialisation of agriculture and the misuse of artificial fertilisers are the factors responsible for this. Cancer is not a matter of fate, but of the environment. It is the murderous tribute we have to pay for industrialisation. V. A. Upton, the former director of the American Cancer Research Center has said, 'Cancer is largely a result of environmental influences. If we can succeed in eliminating these factors, or in reducing them or in bringing them under control, cancer will be avoidable.' We must campaign for a ban on the hard core of carcinogenic compounds (ammonia nitrates, asbestos fibres, benzopyrene, hydrocarbon chlorides etc.).

NUCLEAR POWER AND CANCER

I am being sought
radical mother

mingling in the throng
laying the bomb of fear

I am shedding tear gas
for the power station
future

The trees are still
calendars
meadows are still being
born

But poison clouds are already
driving the heavens away

I see death
rays
over the face of the earth:

the last x-rays
man

Margret Schröder

There are more than 30 million people suffering from
cancer in the industrialised countries every year. In West
Germany 250,000 people develop cancer annually. Official
figures published by German Cancer Aid show that this
includes almost 1,700 children under the age of fifteen. About
4,000 children are receiving steel, radiation or chemical treatment at any one time. These treatments only tackle the
symptoms, but even when it is accepted that the tumour has
already outstripped the body's defence system, they are
common practice. The number of people calling for non-toxic
cancer therapy is on the increase.

The nuclear age has become the cancer age. Appalling
instances of radiation damage are on the increase. My sister
died at the age of ten after suffering radiation treatment. Many
people are now concerned that radioactive substances used on

the patient may be extremely harmful. The number of children who have been damaged by radiation therapy has reached a very worrying level.

Some reports to make one's hair stand on end:

In 1978 the government in Washington declared fifty nuclear installations a health hazard. Statistics show that there was a disproportionately higher incidence of leukaemia and other forms of cancer in these areas than in normal towns and communities. Eliminating the danger would have cost $250 million.

– The Harrisburg Accident: radiation dose unknown. 'Just how much radioactivity escaped during the reactor disaster at the nuclear power station on Three Mile Island is something we shall never know for sure. Gibsen, the investigator, told the United States Atomic Energy Commission that all the radiation meter indicators had gone off the edge of the page that morning. However, about 80 per cent of the radioactivity discharged escaped through the used air chimneys, and the measuring instruments there were not set for radiation emission of that order. The curves also exceeded the upper limits of the measuring scales in the buildings adjacent to the reactor, even though these go up to 1,000 rem per hour. Five rem per annum is the maximum exposure to radiation for workers in power stations.'

– A dispute has been raging in Landshut, Bavaria, since February 1980 over the sudden appearance of white sparrows, many of which are deformed. While the Bavarian Ministry of the Environment and the power station authorities deny any connection, many scientists put it down to radiation leakage from the local nuclear power station.

– There is also the case of the Munich dentist who discovered that some children had radioactive strontium in their teeth. 'Dr Korff noticed that there were always more cases of gum inflammation (stomatitis aphtosa), among children coming into his surgery after a south wind. On closer investigation, it turned out that when there had been a south wind, the radioactive waste from the nearby reactor was dispersed across Munich. Dr Korff then examined teeth extracted from children and established the presence of radioactive strontium. He also established that the radioactive deposits found in the teeth of children born in Eching were twenty-three times the normal level. Dr Korff also observed an increase in unexplained deaths among children as a result of blood diseases. The dentist alerted the authorities, but they have played down his findings and, according to Dr Korff, the

official measurements have been kept secret (*Diagnosen*, 11 July 1978).
 - An investigation carried out by the Director of the County Health
Department in Rocky Flats USA, came to the conclusion that there is
a higher incidence of leukaemia and lung cancer in the vicinity of the
plutonium works. In districts neighbouring the plutonium works there
was a statistically significant increase in the incidence of leukaemia
and twice as many cases of lung cancer as the national average. The
number of miscarriages was also disproportionately high.
 - An increase in the incidence of leukaemia was established in the
vicinity of the La Hague reprocessing plant in France. These statistics
can be obtained from the Health Department in Cherbourg (for the
period 1976–7).
 - In the view of one American scientist, the incident at the Three
Mile Island power station near Harrisburg very probably contributed
to the deaths of several hundred small children. Sternglass, a radiation
scientist at the University of Pittsburgh comes to the conclusion, in a
detailed study, that there was an actual rise in the infant mortality rate
in the area affected by the radioactive cloud discharged at Three Mile
Island. Using data in the Health Department's own publication *Vital
Statistics*, Sternglass shows that infant mortality in Pennsylvania was
almost twice as high in 1979 with 271 deaths (or 18.5 per 1,000), as it
had been in March 1979 (141 or 10.4 per 1,000). At the same time,
the American national average went down from 14.1 to 12.5 per
1,000. Radiologist Sternglass believes that, if their mothers were
living close to the power station, it is possible that the thyroid glands of
unborn children in the fifth to the ninth month in the womb, absorbed
doses of radiation of between 200 and 1,100 millirem. And in areas
where the radioactive cloud touched the ground, Sternglass estimated
that a dose five or ten times higher was possible.

Again, according to *Vital Statistics*, after the Three Mile
Island incident there was an increase in Pennsylvania in the
number of children born alive, yet dying within a few days of
birth, between March (141), May (198) and July (271). There
were similar figures for the city of Pittsburgh, about 290
kilometres to the west of Three Mile Island, and hence in the
path of the radioactive cloud. In the Magee Maternity
Hospital, where 65 per cent of all children in Pittsburgh are
normally born, the infant mortality rate went up from March

(14 deaths per 1,000 births) to May (31.6 deaths per 1,000 births) to July (30.1 deaths per 1,000 births).

– A further study was conducted on the population in the vicinity of the Big Point reactor on Lake Michigan. The results showed that infant mortality was 50 per cent, leukaemia 40 per cent and the incidence of congenital deformities 230 per cent higher than the average for the state of Michigan as a whole.

– In 1975, no less than 998 workers at the Windscale nuclear power station were exposed to quantities of radiation which will mean the loss of many years of life.

– In a study of the Hanford nuclear workers by Dr Alice Stewart and Dr Mancuso, it was established that workers in the nuclear industry receive an annual dose that corresponds to anything between 500 and 5,000 full breast X-rays a year.

It cannot be emphasised enough that the World Health Organisation in Geneva ascribes 80 per cent of all cancer conditions to environmental factors. Health hazards from the food supply are probably much more common than is generally supposed. They arise as a result of industrially produced chemical fertilisers, by using biocides to combat insects, bacteria, weeds and destructive rodents, by deliberate or thoughtless emission of harmful substances by the chemical industry, in the form of harmful substances from the combustion of carbon dioxide and in the release of radioactive gases, condensation, waste air and effluent from nuclear installations. In the view of the experts, the future of cancer relief lies to a large extent in the elimination of these environmental factors.

In October and November 1979, doctors' conferences were held in London, Edinburgh, Copenhagen, Amsterdam and Hamburg on the subject of the dangers of radiation treatment. The participants included leading international scientists, Dr Alice Stewart and Dr George Kneale (UK), Dr Rosalie Bertell (USA) and others. Following increased awareness of the dangers of even low doses of radiation, the maximum permitted levels have been steadily reduced. But now that there are plans to build a large number of fast breeders and re-processing plants all over the world, these levels are being raised again.

An exhaustive statistical study conducted by Dr Stewart showed that children whose mothers had been X-rayed in pregnancy were twice as likely to develop leukaemia. More and more scientists and doctors are warning the population of the dangers of low levels of radiation from nuclear power stations. The dangers of small doses of radioactivity are even recognised by established radiation biologists. The notion of 'harmless tolerance doses' should be dropped.

Notwithstanding these findings, the International Commission on Radiological Protection is recommending a drastic increase in maximum levels. This includes an increase to more than twice the current permitted level of lung exposure to radiation. EURATOM is recommending its member states to accept the new levels because they are necessary for the operation of fast breeders and reprocessing plants. So as not to jeopardise the smooth passage of these efforts, the public will not be informed of the dangers of low levels of radioactive exposure, nor about the further increase in maximum levels.

Meanwhile, Dr Karl Morgan and Professor Rotblatt have issued the following joint statement:

There will never be a complete cure for radiation damage to people; even at a low level of exposure to radiation, many thousands of interactions take place between radiation and human body cells . . . It is clear that if the cell core is damaged and some of the genetic information units are lost, or if a similar set of circumstances leads to malignancy, no dose can be set so low that there is a nil risk. Thus the risk of an outbreak of cancer as a result of the effects of radioactivity increases in more or less direct proportion to the increase or accumulation of radioactive treatment.

There is no threshold of safety; the effects of radiation on the body mount up from one treatment to the next.

Statements which seek to play down the pressures on the environment caused by nuclear installations are irresponsible. Professor Dr Schellong, Director of the University Children's Hospital in Münster, is right in saying that

'the introduction of a legal requirement to register cancer conditions and congenital abnormalities is essential if we are to establish the incidence, and possible fluctuation in incidence, of these conditions. Parliament and Government should make this matter one of urgent priority, especially as the use of nuclear energy is being developed at great speed, despite all the unresolved problems and despite the misgivings of wide sectors of the population.'

The risk of developing cancer from low doses of radiation is evidently much greater than we had ever supposed.

THE CHILDREN'S PLANET

My sister, Grace Patricia Kelly, was not yet eleven years old when she died of cancer. She suffered from carcinoma of the eye. Grace came through four operations. In one of them, her right eye was removed. During her three years of radiation therapy, she spent many weeks in cancer hospitals, far away from her mother, her father and her sisters and brothers. She was on her own, surrounded by adult cancer patients with little sympathy for the sufferings and fears of a dying child.

Following the death of my courageous sister, I began campaigning for improvements in the situation of children suffering from cancer and other chronic diseases. Whilst discovering the dangers of radiation treatment for cancer, I became increasingly concerned about the wider menace of nuclear power.

Splitting the atom; uncontrollable emission of radioactive toxins; the insanity of the nuclear, bacteriological and chemical weapons build-up; unrestrained economic growth spreading commercialisation to every aspect of our lives; overconsumption of goods and raw materials; the erosion of the individual's right to free speech; anti-human architecture, transport, technology and food production; increasing indifference and irresponsibility on the political front – these are the conditions of modern industrial society, and these are the factors responsible for disease. In an epoch characterized by 'gorging to excess' all sense of responsibility has disappeared. Cancer has become a fitting symbol for the disease of civilised society. Shall we let ourselves be turned into cancer cells, gorging our way to self-gratification, all caution thrown to the winds?

Since following and experiencing my sister's suffering as a cancer patient in those cold, loveless hospitals and radiation clinics, time and again, I have witnessed the way in which 'medical progress' is itself a cause of illness. Ivan Illich has already proved that in the industrialised countries life expectancy is stagnating, or even falling, despite the cost explosion in the health services.

One of the main features of modern science, including medical science, is a tendency to reduce reality to a level which can be calculated in a laboratory or predicted by the computer. People have been reduced to finite objects, and human characteristics, such as creativity, imagination, hope and disappointment, simply do not figure any more. There is almost no better place to observe this reduction of human beings than in a modern hospital.

While there has been an over-emphasis on technology in medicine in the last few years, at the same time there has also been greater public awareness of the psychological causes of ill-health. The growing trend towards homoeopathic medicines shows that, especially in the field of health, people want a more human approach to science and technology, one that does not separate body from soul.

The stubborn attitudes encountered in many hospitals

underline the inhumanity of medical science. It has long been known that four out of five children react to being separated from their parents by being disruptive, stuttering, bed-wetting, having nightmares or loss of sleep and appetite. But hospitals will only permit mothers to stay on with their children in exceptional circumstances. Shortage of space is one reason for this; the absurdly high daily charges another. Some of the hospital administrators I have spoken to responded to this miserable state of affairs by saying that patients will just have to learn to live with it. Just as we have long since got used to hostile tower blocks and a polluted environment?

Cancer patients in particular are treated as though they were the lepers of the modern age. Take a man who has had a heart attack to illustrate the point. He is often regarded with something verging on admiration because he has obviously been working too hard, and that really counts for something in our work-mad society. But none of that applies to cancer. The word 'cancer' arouses almost medieval fears of the awful, the unknown, the terrifying. Cancer sufferers often encounter ignorance, fear and stupidity. The uncaring attitude and the unconscious prejudices many people have about cancer victims are often more painful than the condition itself.

Given that after accidents, cancer is the second most common cause of death in children in Europe, various organisations have put forward the idea of special centres for children with cancer. These include a working group in the European section of the World Health Organisation and the private organisation I founded, the *Grace P. Kelly Association for the Support of Research into Children's Cancer*.

The need for these centres hinges on the way body and soul are separated in methods of treatment and therapy, such as operations, radiation treatment and chemical therapy where important questions are left out: how are cancer wards furnished? what effect does the general arrangement of the room and the daily routine have on the small patient? are there enough properly trained nursing staff on hand to tend to the child's emotional problems?

My sister Grace often told me about the tears that were shed in the neighbouring beds, and how other young cancer patients suffered boredom, bouts of anxiety, apathy and withdrawal. Her example of a child's courage and honesty has given me all the inspiration, strength and energy I have needed since her death to found and publicise an association, a European action group, which aims to improve the lot of children with cancer.

After my sister's death, I helped found a European association which aims to represent the interests of children suffering from cancer or other chronic illnesses in the increasingly depersonalised atmosphere of the hospital. The Grace P. Kelly Association uses its funds not only to promote cancer research, but also to encourage cooperation across Europe. We hope to construct a European model of cancer treatment which stresses the social aspects, both in psychological and paediatric terms. We call our project the Children's Planet, and it represents an autonomous world of children, with no white coats and no hierarchies, where children need no longer feel like outcasts.

The idea of the Children's Planet is based on the world described in *The Little Prince* by St.-Exupéry. A team of very committed planners and architects have drawn up plans for a Children's Planet of this kind, in consultation with doctors and psychologists. We have spent years closely examining the specific problems of children with cancer and other chronic diseases, and I have visited many children's hospitals in Europe and the United States to learn from other examples of clinical care, nursing supervision and leisure activities.

The Children's Planet's main concern will be research into the various ways in which chronically sick children can live with their pain, how they behave and react. It will consist of the following areas: firstly, a large work-space for outpatients where group therapy can take place and therapies can be supervised; secondly, a model 'rooming-in' area where children who need time to adjust to their treatment can be looked after by their mothers or fathers; thirdly, a home dialysis training centre where children with chronic kidney disorders should be able to develop a degree of independence; and fourthly, a hospital school, with a large play and activities area. The first three areas will all be grouped round the fourth, a centrally situated play and activities pavillion. In this area, sick children will be able to do craft work, play in the sandpit, splash around in water, make and listen to music, read, act in plays and so on. Children will wait for their treatment here, and children who have already been admitted to hospital as in-patients will come over to play. It will also be a kindergarten for the children of hospital staff. The play area will consist of a large, flexible hall with distinct spaces within it and a pyramid-shaped superstructure. The hall will be lit by natural light through a large number of windows to the outside world. Team games will be played in an adjacent open play area as well as in the central play/activities area. The visual impression will be of an open hall and a distinctive play and work shop.

The small patients' active involvement and participation in the Children's Planet should help them to bear their dreadful suffering and to take an active part in their own therapy.

To the Adult Reader:
You say:
'Looking after children
is tiring.'
You are right.
You say:
'Because we have to
stoop to their level.
Climb down, lean down to them,
bend, make ourselves smaller.'

You are wrong.
That is not what's tiring. What is,
is having to clamber up to their feelings.
Clamber up, stretch out, stand on tip toes,
reach out,
to avoid hurt.

Janusz Korczak

LIFE AND DEATH IN MY OWN BODY

I have had personal experience of the way in which our belief in progress can destroy love and life. Since the age of six, I have had many X-rays in connection with a number of kidney operations. In 1978 I lost a child in the sixth week of pregnancy. The foetus was damaged and my own state of health deteriorated severely. I shall never be able to prove that it was caused by the X-rays but it is a question I shall go on asking. The same doctors who claim that nuclear power stations are safe, also tend to say that X-rays will not prevent mothers having healthy children. In the period following my brief pregnancy, I read the words of the Chilean poet, Gabriela Mistral, with tears in my eyes, and with great apprehension.

I place roses on my body and recite unending
verses to the being reposing within me.
Hour upon hour in my arbour, I drink in
the blazing sun.
Like a fruit, I want to trickle honey
deep down into my innermost self.
I turn my face to the wind of the pine-groves.
Light and wind shall colour and cleanse my blood.

To make it even purer, I avoid all hate
and all gossip –
I want only to love!
For I am weaving a life,
in this peace and quiet,
a wonderful life,
with veins and countenance and expressions
and a purified heart.

For I am weaving a life in this peace and quiet . . . Yet where is the peace, where is the quiet?

I read the sad balance sheet: the number of unwanted pregnancies generally exceeds the number of wanted ones. The reasons? Often socio-economic but sometimes purely medical.

Who is there to offer aid and comfort when a pregnancy endangers the expectant mother's health or when the embryo is at risk? Who is telling the real truth about the risk of a severe handicap or abnormality in the unborn child? Who can reassure me that exposure to radiation as a result of frequent X-rays did not harm the genetic product in my womb? In the Federal Republic of Germany, there are approximately 200,000 damaged children in every million live births and the numbers are increasing. And so are nuclear weapons tests, the military and peaceful use of nuclear energy, diagnostic X-rays and carcinogenic pollutants.

Handicapped children require constant care from the moment they are born until they die. Generally, mothers have to carry these burdens on their own and in private; their own lives are completely taken over and destroyed.

While there is a shortage of ante-natal clinics, over 50 per cent of all scientists work on military projects. 400,000 of them are directly employed in the development of new weapons.

For six weeks, my life was dominated by one question, were all the X-rays I had to have over the last few years an acceptable risk? Was there an additional exposure to radiation when I took Grace, my little sister, to the Heidelberg Radiation Clinic? Did my visits to nuclear reactors have a negative effect on my body? How high is, or was, the level of radiation in Belgium where I was living at the time? Is there an accumulation of fall-out from nuclear tests in fish, grain and ruminants? Is there an expert on radiological protection who will tell me the truth about my embryo? Is there such a thing as a 'tolerable' dose of radiation? And if such a thing is permitted, who gave permission for it?

The International Commission on Radiological Protection is often mentioned; it is the body that sets the guidelines for the genetic risk of radiation to the population. But what about the embryo, the unborn child? They are a great deal more susceptible to radiation than after birth or as adults. People are not susceptible to radiation to the same degree. Why are we not told the truth?

There were not many answers for me then, nor are there many for me now. The doctors, men and women, gave me no hope at all that the little baby I carried for six weeks would be born healthy.

Embryonic tissue are the most radiation-sensitive of all tissue. I have had many X-rays of the pelvis, the kidneys and the abdomen. And as a result, I put a tiny embryo, a human life at risk.

The verdict was announced: the continuation of the pregnancy would endanger the health of both mother and child. Nobody could give me any assurance that we, the embryo and I, would come through everything after all. Yet every day, the government and the nuclear industry issue blithe statements that we need have no fear of nuclear power stations, reprocessing plants or the disposal of nuclear waste. Everything is in apple-pie order – except my womb! And so I was forced to sacrifice the embryo and cannot join Gabriela Mistral in her song.* I can only weep . . . weep about an operation that might not have been necessary, had we not permitted permission to be given.

Radioactivity as a by-product of civilisation – yes, I am frightened! But then on the other hand, maybe I saved a child from a future nuclear holocaust . . . It lives on in me as my unseen ombudsman of the unborn. But I can never weave a life again.

These experiences brought it home to me that we are all victims of ecological atrocity. Posing the question of a new order of society may seem unrealistic, utopian or even dangerous to many people. But, at the threshold of the most dangerous decade of our history, it is simply a question of survival. If there is any hope, it must depend on a new way of thinking, and a new way of taking action. We must spike the lies of political life, and surmount every constraint. We must mount an international general strike against war and the nuclear industry.

* I am told that although childbirth was a frequent theme in Gabriela Mistral's work, she did not, in fact, ever have any children of her own – MH.

PART 6 Women and Ecology

WHILE WOMEN HAVE INCREASINGLY DISCOVERED their own oppression in Western Europe, in the United States, in Australia and elsewhere, they have also learned to organise themselves and to speak out against the oppression of others – particularly the victims of militarisation and nuclearisation.

There has been much consciousness raising among the new brave women in a 'brave new world'. Political issues become personal, and personal issues become political. I have been with many women, whether I marched alongside them in Sydney or Hiroshima or Whyl, whether I sat in a tent on a windy Irish day at Carnsore Point, or spoke to them at the UN Plaza during the Disarmament March, or during my campaign trail for the European Elections as head of the German Ecological List.

I have hope for the world, although it is ten minutes before Doomsday. Women all over the world are rising up, and infusing the anti-nuclear and peace movements with a vitality and creativity never seen before. Women stand up in court-rooms and explain the differences between natural and arti-ficial radiation; they stand up at demonstrations and non-violent occupations of nuclear sites. They are the genuine ombudsmen of children to come. Like Dr Helen Coldicott, a children's doctor from Australia, they firmly believe that each of us must accept total responsibility for the earth's survival.

We are discovering how commercial and military techno-logies impose unacceptable risks to health and life. To defeat these technologies, we must begin to shape world events.

World expenditure on the arms race is over $1,000 million per day. Countless children are condemned to illiteracy, disease, starvation and death by the massive diversion of resources (natural and human) to the arms race. The cost of one tank would supply equipment for 520 classrooms and the cost of one destroyer could provide electrification for three cities and nineteen rural zones. Women who have opposed the military base enlargement in Larzac, women who do not buy toy guns at Christmas, know that the accumulation of weapons today constitutes much more of a threat than a protection. There had been over 900 nuclear explosions on the surface of the earth by the end of 1978 and it is estimated that the number of soldiers in the world today is twice the number of teachers, doctors and nurses.

Woman must lead the efforts in education for peace awareness, because only she, I feel, can go back to her womb, her roots, her natural rhythms, her inner search for harmony and peace, while men, most of them anyway, are continually bound to their power struggle, the exploitation of nature, and military ego trips. Our timidity must end for the earth has no emergency exit.

The conditions are being created for a police state, centralized uncontrollable energy systems, and increasing mechanization all led by the silicon chip which Japanese manufacturers claim achieves circuits in which there only are thirty failures in one billion hours of operation. Increasing numbers of persons will become unemployed and superfluous – already in 1970, in a report to the World Bank, Robert McNamara spoke of such persons as 'marginal men'. It is estimated that by 1980, there will be one billion of them. The huge corporations that make human beings marginal can sell, make and break governments, and decide whether a non-nuclear nation like Ireland will have to go nuclear. And the same big companies now even begin to dominate the solar industry in the West. According to UN reports, a new form of so-called solar monopoly could mean further Third World dependence on a handful of corporations. Already production of large solar-based electricity generating plants is mainly restricted to gigantic companies like Northrup, McDonnell-Douglas and Mobil Oil. The Ford Motor Corporation, Philips and General Motors dominate small and medium-sized solar power plants. Firms are attempting to restrict access to this technology – awaiting the time when they need areas of *cheap* labour before moving production out to the Third World.

We are often told, that the experts and the big firms do not know how to deal with the problems which threaten world-wide disaster, 'that all the facts are not in,' that more research must be done, and more reports written. This is simply an excuse for endlessly putting off action. We already know enough to begin to deal with all our major problems: nuclear war, over-population, pollution, hunger, the desolation of the planet, the inequality among peoples. The present crisis is a crisis not of information, but of policy. We cannot cope with all the problems that threaten us, while maximising profits.

As things stand now, the people, especially women and children of the Third World, are to perish first. They have already begun to starve; all that is asked of them is to starve quietly. The plight of women in the Third World is one that touches me deeply. There are now about 100 million children under the age of five always hungry. Each year 15 million children die from infection and malnutrition. There are about 800 million illiterates in the world, nearly two-thirds of them are women.

The number of women unable to read and write is about half a billion. In the Third World, 40–70 per cent of agricultural labour is female – they plant the seed, haul the water, tend the animals, strive to keep their families alive – but all the while they are socially inferior. Men in the Third World are lured into the cities to work for one of the many Western companies or join Third World armies, supplied with guns and tanks sold by the same companies. The women left behind on the land, usually infibulated and circumcised (bodily and sexually mutilated), are not taught the use of new irrigation systems and intermediate small scale alternative technology. Instead they learn to buy Nestle's Lactogen Milk Powder to mix with dirty brown water. The result: many babies die with bloated stomachs. Women in the Third World are further exploited through various forms of prostitution – whether through 'rent-a-wife' schemes, as in Vietnam, or through international finance companies developing hotel brothels and promoting tourism through sexist advertisements.

The developed nations are armed to the teeth and mean not only to hold on to what they have, but to grasp anything they still can. Look at the uranium mines in Namibia, look at what we, the Europeans, are doing to the soul and culture of the Aborigines in Australia; look at the plight of the Navajo Indians in North America dying from radon gases. And as the great famines occur, the grain and other agricultural produce is either rotting away in EEC silos or is fed to cattle to supply the rapidly increasing demand for meat in affluent countries. The suffering people of this world must come together to take control of their lives, to wrest political power from their present masters, who are pushing them towards destruction.

This is also a plea to all women to join those sisters who have already risen up – who have helped to shape the ecological revolution. Together we can overthrow all the imposed structures of domination.

Even in the affluent parts of the world the same patterns of sexual inequality may be seen. Equal pay and equal treatment in all areas of schooling, training, promotion and working conditions have not, in reality, been won. Women in South Italy, and in the West of Ireland lead lives of desperation and humiliation. Battered women and children take refuge from husbands and fathers and women increasingly get cervical cancers and other abnormalities from the Pill of the pharmaceutical giants. Women who stay on hormones poison their cells, saturate their bile and risk birth defects in later children. Every eighth child in Germany is born handicapped in some way.

The story of thalidomide, commercially available for years after it should have been outlawed, is just one of many. The pitiful caricatures of adults, living reminders of an unconcerned pharmacology, show how lethal the policies of male researchers and male politicians have been – industries have falsified data, bought off scientists, posited ridiculous risk-benefit ratios and threshold levels. This has resulted in a cancer rate that qualifies as 'epidemic'. The total economic impact – including health care and lost productivity due to cancer – has been estimated at $25 billion a year.

The earth has been mistreated, and only by restoring a balance, only by living *with* the earth, by employing soft energies and soft technologies can we overcome the violence of patriarchy. Although the masculine ego and capitalist consciousness have made advances in science and technology, they have lost touch with the earth in setting out to conquer nature. The desire for power has left in its wake a terrible path of destruction. There is at the same time a danger of women being seen in the subservient role from which they hope to rise. Some of the ecological, communal and human potential movements are deeply infected by a type of romantic escapism which could all too easily recreate woman's role as the servant of male culture. As an English feminist once said 'We don't want an ecological society where men build windmills and women silently listen, bake bread and weave rugs.'

In recent years, I have also observed that some women have sought to overcome their inferior role by becoming part of the masculine world (Mrs Thatcher, Indira Gandhi, etc.). When women fight for equal status with men, they run the risk of joining the ranks in times of war. We are so conditioned by masculine values that women often make the mistake of imitating and emulating men at the cost of their own feminism. When I assess the world of male values, it is clear to me that I do not want this kind of 'equality'.

Recent court-martial proceedings in the USA have indicated that a large group of guardsmen responsible for nuclear missiles are using and distributing illegal drugs. Armed guards had used marijuana, cocaine and LSD while on duty and carrying a loaded pistol. Another example of wanton disregard for life is provided by the French electricity generating board, which recently decided to bring into operation two new nuclear power stations while admitting that there are certain cracks in key reactor components. While governments all over the world are faced with escalating nuclear research bills (bills, which private industry will *not* pick up), and while workers repair nuclear accidents with pencils and paper clips (as was recently the case in a nuclear station in Virginia) a young woman is shot dead by the police in an anti-nuclear demonstration in Spain; policemen denounce women as 'whores' during pro-abortion demonstrations and there are still investigations going on to discover what really happened to Karen Silkwood.

1984 is nearly here and so are the police states foreseen by Orwell – all in the name of secure nuclear societies. Women must lose all fear of speaking up and demanding what is theirs and their children's. Only if we begin to rediscover our own nature, can we discover new ways of wholeness, balance, and decentralisation – can we forge a bond with the Earth and the Moon, living with cooperation, gentleness, non-possessiveness and soft energies.

PART 7 For an Erotic Society

ALL TOO OFTEN, WE ALLOW OURSELVES TO BE TAKEN
in by an abundant assortment of images in which love is
ever more distorted. In our society, men and women are led
astray by access to commercialised sexuality, escapism and
jealousy. Loving demands a great effort on our part. We are
all aware of this, yet so many of us find ourselves in flight
together.

In our society, love – the mystical dimension of life where the
worlds of the spiritual and the physical are united – has been
absorbed into the mechanical world of production; love has
been reduced either to performance, or to consumer goods.
We have reached a point where people want to 'have' without
being prepared to 'give', or simply to 'be'.

The main obstacle to love is its over-idealization. It is indeed
one of our aims to find love, yet we doubt our own ability
to achieve this. We must make a start on love and eroticism
where they are a reality, where we actually appreciate them –
in our daily lives. We must make love a reality here and now.

Even in progressive political circles I come up against
barriers when I talk of the religious character of love, and the
erotic character of genuine religious feeling. The inner relationship between religious mysticism, spiritual love and physical eroticism derives from the fact that, by its nature, the true
erotic transcends the confines of the ego, leading to a transcendental, mystic experience. The supra-personal quality of love
is communicated to us naturally, in the personality of the
individual whom one loves. We should always remain aware of
the supra-personal dimension. The erotic element released
between two people who love one another creates something
beyond either one of them, extending their horizons. All too
often, I come across men and women in our movement who
shrink from the freedom afforded by love and eroticism
because of their own personal disappointments. The (political
and personal) 'ideology' that they espouse is not prepared to

admit to anything that cannot be rationally explained. Everything that is loving is suspect.

In today's nuclear, militarised world, almost all human relationships are riddled with suspicion, anxiety and insecurity. Love cannot emerge triumphant and unambiguous in a system of 'fall-back' positions and restrictions. Conformity and submission are just two items in the emotional currency of this materialist society. We will continue to fail in our ability to love until we recognize that it is the personal responsibility of each individual to learn how to love. As women we must vigorously oppose all attempts to deny a place for the imagination in love, and we must strive for the harmonious interaction of the physical and the intellectual and spiritual. In a world where practically everything is planned, where everything is seen and valued in terms of its utility, the erotic must become the spiritual dimension of our physical being.

Leafing through books on Tantra temples, art and Tantra yoga, and reading about love relationships in Taoism and the early matriarchal societies, I am struck by the fact that we have lost a culture of love, or what Adorno calls 'the aroma of the erotic'. All too often, encounters between the sexes amount to nothing more than sheer sexuality – individual gratification, the impatience some men have about entering their partner, advertising of aids to increase stimulation, and sexual acrobatics. Creative attention to the form and force of our own eroticism is disappearing fast and relationships have lost much of their excitement.

Setting up as a couple can be a grave mistake when a selfish need for security means that one partner stands in the way of change and development. Love is not an isolated romantic act between two people; love and life are indissolubly linked with one another. Love must be an integral part of all areas of society, so that it can halt the forward march of isolation, separation and a hostile social order.

TANTRA-TAOISM-LIBERATION

The erotic is an elemental revolutionary force. It can suspend existing forms of discontinuity so as to arrive at continuity, entirety and a fuller, deeper way of life.

The melting and flowing into one another of the erotic can take place at various levels of sexuality. It does not have to be exclusively male–female oriented. More and more women are rejecting heterosexuality either for a short period or on a permanent basis and are seeking to arrive at a new awareness of their own sexuality and their own bodies in their relationships. Some do not want to share this most intimate area solely with men, and include women in their emotional life; others do not want men to enter them during the fertile days of their cycles, or even at all. Some use the most natural contraception method of all. This represents a *new form of sexuality*. Mutual satisfaction and one's own fulfillment, are not some kind of substitute; many of us enjoy them a great deal more. There are many parts of the body where you can have an orgasm.

We must be on our guard lest the ideology of 'free sexuality and emancipation' and all the bland propaganda there has been for the Pill despite its dangers subject us even more to male pressures. We women have been brought up to conform and to take a passive role, especially in terms of our own sexuality. Our sexuality has always been defined in terms of the penis. Men, including liberated ones, are brought up to be strong, and to measure their potency by the size of their penis and the frequency and timing of their ejaculations. In the Western world, sexual togetherness is restricted to particular erogenous zones. What has happened to touching, to caresses? In the erotic, non-violent, loving society that I would like to see, people will expect more than a simple capacity for sex. The most common complaint that women make of men is that they are totally unaware of the fact that the woman is not experiencing or feeling anything – the man is always in too much of a hurry to enter the woman. And that men tend to regard intense complete sexual unison and *spiritual* readiness for love, as an unnecessary diversion from their own fulfilment. The tendency to regard sexual intercourse exclusively in penis-related terms, and to cut ourselves off from all other aspects of this 'melting into one another' leads to all sorts of misunderstandings, and can have an increasingly destructive effect on the love relationship. In next to no time, the result is that one partner is being used and the ability to love is put at risk.

A view of *sexuality* as a 'technical acrobatic *performance*' is most certainly not the nub of a genuine love relationship; the nub is rather the ability to achieve a living, mutual relationship, one that is anchored in the spiritual, where the erotic may rise above the 'confines of self' and thus lead to a mystical transcendental experience. I agree with David Cooper (*On the Need for Freedom*) that 'The simplistic view that the man is there to penetrate the woman is a culturally conditioned belief that is easily refuted by experience.'

For example, Tantric yoga is based on *mutual* penetration, and the conflict between penetrator and penetrated is removed. There is a very great need to touch and hold and explore one another, instead of just penetrate!

We must not be ruled by our heads and our polluted perceptions. We must experience the mystic dimensions of life, in which *mind and sensuality* do not stand in one another's way and are, in fact, indissolubly united. We must find our way back to a way of life we thought we had lost.

In erotic ecstasy, the intellectual and the sensual can never be separated. According to Tantric yoga, man is a never-ending spiritual creature and the melting together of man and woman is akin to the divine act of creation. It is thus possible to achieve the supreme state of existence through an intense act of physical love. Tantricism not only contributes to an appreciation of individual sexuality, it also shows the way out of the fragmentation of modern man by means of a complementary conception of body and spirit (man and woman).

If love predominates at *all* levels, man will no longer be pre-occupied with attempts, motivated by contempt and hate, to change people and things by means of punishment. Love which leads to ecstasy also leads to clarity and peace. It heals the wounds of separation and lends man dignity.

What once amounted to nothing more than a manipulation of organs now becomes an awareness of love – love that indeed transforms, but is *not* demanding, allowing us to develop our own awareness of the meaning of life. Being back in the world again, after this free melting into one another, gives a feeling of inner security. We are no longer a 'thing in the world'; we have become the 'embodiment of the world'. Tantricism seeks to lead man to his real being and has several possible levels: intensively lived love; physical eroticism; eroticism of the heart; holy eros! Yearning for wholeness!

This is expressed in exactly the same way in ecstatic Buddhism and Chinese Taoism. In the latter, the central symbol is the revolving wheel with two fish-shaped sacs within it: yin and yang. Unlimited endlessness. Each of these two forces carries some of its opposite within itself.

JEALOUSY AND FIDELITY

Whenever love comes up against rules and restrictions, it is as though it were shut in a cage where it becomes the ugliest thing in the world. When lovers fight, the tragedy is that they demand too much of one another. Jealousy, possessiveness, suspicion and pettiness – all have their origin in an attitude of hostility to love and in the way society is structured on competition. An inner ideal of love is on a total collision course with the actual state of communication in this society. The trust we desire disintegrates in the face of fail-safe and fall-back strategies, and ways of thinking and responding come to the fore which are diametrically opposed to love.

Sexual fidelity in a relationship between two people can be a meaningful – and sometimes essential – decision, constructured in competition.

Sexual fidelity in a relationship between two people can be a meaningful – and sometimes essential – decision when consciously and freely entered into by both parties. But as an absolute principle, it can be just as destructive as promiscuity can. I believe that human beings are not exclusively monogamous, and that this should always be taken into account.

There is a world of difference between a free choice to renounce all involvement outside a relationship, and a ban on such involvement. The pressure to make rules, the suspicion and the need for guarantees, in other words the 'jealousy syndrome', has a great deal to do with a *fear of being dispensable.* This arises from the structure of our commercialised society where people value each other according to the qualities and abilities they contribute to the human market. Men and women are constantly being compared with potential rivals. They live with latent feelings of inferiority.

Nena and George O'Neill have come up with a new definition of fidelity. In its original sense, fidelity meant sticking to a duty or obligation. In the O'Neill's concept of open marriage, it is not psychological dependence that welds the partners together, but rather a sense of responsibility towards the other partner's growth, the integrity of self and mutual respect.

For myself, it has become abundantly clear that the more harmoniously and self-confidently one lives with oneself, the more one can love, admit to liberty and share in the growth of one's partner. In a partnership where each is sure of his or her own identity and each trusts the other, there will always be space for additional relationships. These can always have a vitalising and enriching effect on an *open partnership*.

If our aims as women are to make our own decisions and to find our own fulfilment, we cannot exclude sexuality. In 1886, Eleanor Marx-Aveling wrote, 'There will no longer be one right for women and another for men. If future society, such as current European society, allows men the right to have a mistress as well as a wife, then we can be certain that this kind of freedom will be extended to women.' How few of us have managed to live in relationships that were truly free and emotionally and sexually fulfilling without fidelity. Love relationships must be liberated from the desire for possession and domination.

Alexandra Kollontai (1872–1952) is very dear to my heart. In her life and work, she demonstrated that complete surrender to, and love for, a man do not have to be the focal point of a woman's life. The focus should be one's *own* work, one's *own* achievement and the self-confidence awakened by it. 'The new woman does not want to be exclusive property where she loves. Because she demands respect for the freedom of her own feelings, she learns to permit this in other people . . . In the new woman, the human being is triumphing more and more over the jealous little woman.' She sums up her sketch of the 'new woman' in this way:

Self-discipline in place of emotional outbursts, an ability to appreciate her own freedom and independence in place of impersonal submissiveness, the assertion of her own individuality in place of naive attempts to adopt and reflect the 'alien model' of the loved one. The open display of the right to family happiness, instead of the hypocritical mask of imperviousness and relegation of the experiences of love to an unimportant place in life. We no longer have before us the 'little woman', the pale shadow of the man – what we have is the personality, the woman as a person.

Alexandra Kollontai's stories and her life show that work and the desire for love can be combined in harmony with one another. At the same time, they reveal the importance for women's liberation of inner freedom and independence. For me personally, the harmony between passion and spiritual closeness, the accord of love with liberty and of friendship with independence are the greatest ideal. I know from my own experience that love can only flourish in the freedom and spontaneity of one's own feelings, and that life may be rich in the experience of love, if men and women are both free to make their own decisions.

ABOUT THE AUTHOR

Petra Karin Kelly was born on 27 November 1947 in Günzburg/Danube. She owes her English surname to her stepfather, John E. Kelly, who for many years was an American Army Officer, an Irish American who worked in the hospital service. She was first educated in Günzburg where she attended a Catholic girls' boarding school but went to the United States in 1960 where she attended High School in Georgia and Virginia. From 1966–1970 she studied World Politics and International Relations in the School of International Service at the American University, Washington, and graduated with a BA *cum laude*. She taught for a year at the same university, which has a high proportion of foreign students, and received a Woodrow Wilson Fellowship. During this period, she also worked as a volunteer in the offices of Senators Robert Kennedy and Hubert Humphrey in their election campaigns, and was founder and chairperson of 'International Week', a series of provocative seminars and lectures on international politics in Washington D.C.

From 1970–71 she studied Political Science and European Integration at the University of Amsterdam and also worked as a research assistant at the Europa Institute until October 1971. She was awarded her Masters degree (MA) at the end of her period of study in Amsterdam.

She first started work at the European Communities in Brussels in 1971 as an EEC intern in the cabinet of Attiero Spinelli and in the General Secretariat, followed by a six months' research bursary (*Bourse de Recherche*) in 1972. During this period, she had a scholarship to study the political concerns and aims of the various European movements and groupings from 1945–70. In 1972–3 she worked as a European civil servant with the Economic and Social Committee of the EEC and worked on questions of vocational training, itinerant workers, equal pay and general labour and health questions. From October 1973 on, she was appointed administrator in the Secretariat of the Economic and Social Committee, dealing with social questions, environmental protection, health and education at the EEC in Brussels.

In addition to her professional activities, Petra Kelly has been active in the European women's, peace and anti-nuclear movements. While still in the United States she took part in demonstrations against the Vietnam War and nuclear bombs. After the death of her ten-year old sister, Grace Patricia, from cancer in 1970, she founded the 'Grace P. Kelly Association for the Support of Research into Children's Cancer', an independent citizens' action group which has developed a psycho-social model for the care of children with cancer or other chronic diseases (Children's Planet), and includes in its work investigation of the causes of cancer in children living in the vicinity of chemical and nuclear installations.

In 1972 she joined the West German Association of Environmental Protection Action Groups (BBU) and from 1979–1980 was the federal committee member responsible for international contacts. She joined the Social Democratic Party of Germany when Willy Brandt was Chancellor, but left it at the beginning of 1979 in protest against policies on nuclear defence, health and women. She left, also, to build up the Green Party with several friends. She became active in various bodies such as the German Peace Society/Association of Conscientious Objectors, the Humanist Union, and various centres for education and non-violent action.

Having become closely acquainted with, and an active supporter of, the ecology, women's and peace movements at home and abroad, she helped to found the Greens in 1979 and was their leading national candidate in the European elections, in which the Greens received 3.2 per cent of the West German vote. Then, in 1980, she ran as head of the Bavarian List; in

1982, as head of the Regional List (Bavarian Elections); and, in 1983, as head of the Bavarian List again in the Federal Elections. In March 1980, she was elected one of the three spokesmen of the Federal Executive Committee of the Greens. In November 1982, she left this post in accordance with the Greens regulations on the rotation of responsibilities. She was awarded the Alternative Nobel Prize, established by Jahob von Uexküll, in Stockholm in December 1982. And, in 1983, she was awarded the Peace Woman of the Year Award in America by the organisation, Women Strike for Peace.

Following the West German elections in March 1983, Petra Kelly was one of the twenty-seven Greens elected to the *Bundestag*. There she was elected one of the Greens three parliamentary speakers.

Petra Kelly, has published several books and many articles in English and German on ecology, feminism, children's cancer, disarmament and Hiroshima. Among them are *Lasst uns die Kraniche suchen* (Let us Search for the Cranes) and *A Nuclear Ireland?* (with John F. Carroll of the Irish Transport and General Workers Union).

◆

About South End Press

South End Press is a nonprofit, collectively run book publisher with more than 200 titles in print. Since our founding in 1977, we have tried to meet the needs of readers who are exploring, or are already committed to, the politics of radical social change. Our goal is to publish books that encourage critical thinking and constructive action on the key political, cultural, social, economic, and ecological issues shaping life in the United States and in the world. In this way, we hope to give expression to a wide diversity of democratic social movements and to provide an alternative to the products of corporate publishing.

Through the Institute for Social and Cultural Change, South End Press works with other political media projects—Z Magazine; Speakout, a speakers' bureau; and Alternative Radio—to expand access to information and critical analysis.

To order books, please send a check or money order to: South End Press, 7 Brookline Street, #1, Cambridge, MA 02139-4146. To order by credit card, call 1-800-533-8478. Please include $3.50 for postage and handling for the first book and 50 cents for each additional book. Write or e-mail southend@southendpress.org for a free catalog, or visit our web site: http://www.southendpress.org.